THE MULTIPLE FUTURES
OF CAPITALISM

A Convoco Edition

CORINNE MICHAELA FLICK (ED.)

Convoco! Editions

Convoco Foundation
Brienner Strasse 28
D – 80333 Munich
www.convoco.co.uk

British Library Cataloguing-in-Publication data: a catalogue
record for this book is available from the British Library.

Edited by Dr. Corinne Michaela Flick
Translated from German by Philippa Hurd
Layout and typesetting by Jill Sawyer Phypers
Printed and bound in Great Britain by Clays Ltd., St Ives plc

ISBN: 978-0-9931953-8-9

Previously published Convoco titles:

The Common Good in the 21st Century (2018)

Authority in Transformation (2017)

Power and its Paradoxes (2016)

To Do or Not To Do—Inaction as a Form of Action (2015)

Dealing with Downturns: Strategies in Uncertain Times (2014)

Collective Law-Breaking—A Threat to Liberty (2013)

Who Owns the World's Knowledge? (2012)

**Can't Pay, Won't Pay? Sovereign Debt and the Challenge of
Growth in Europe (2011)**

The political problem of mankind is to combine
three things: economic efficiency, social justice,
and individual liberty.

John Maynard Keynes (1883–1946)

CONTENTS

INTRODUCTION

Dear Friends of Convoco,

It is always a gamble to address a topic dealing with the future. Things to come are always uncertain and depend on many factors, which can often be predicted only to a limited extent, and usually not at all. Today especially, in our rapidly changing world, everything seems more unpredictable than ever. However, in order to do justice to the topic of capitalism, we must put the future at the heart of our discussion. Future-orientation is inherent to capitalism. On the one hand, its very existence is based on looking ahead—investments are made today so that we can benefit from them tomorrow. Without forward-looking strategies and expectations, the capitalist system would not be able to function. On the other hand, looking to the future is one way of helping to shape the paths that capitalism will take. Imagining things to come means exerting an influence on them, for concepts and visions set the direction of development. Visions are crucial management tools for transforming existing conditions.

The focus of this volume is the question of how capitalism must change in order to remain a successful model for our society. It is a matter of thinking about how capitalism needs to alter so that more people can participate in or benefit from it. Fundamentally, we must be aware that capitalism works only when there are enough successful people who can continue to be consumers, to the extent that they transform economic opportunities into ways of living. In this way, inhabitants become citizens.

We have chosen the word "capitalism" deliberately. It is ideologically freighted, inviting contradiction the moment you hear it. Those who find the term too ideologically charged can replace it with the value-neutral term of "market economy." In a classical definition, capitalism means radical subservience to the laws of the market. This idea can be traced back to the political economist and philosopher Adam Smith. His book, *The Wealth of Nations*, is the basis of our current system. Adam Smith is the first economist to place markets at the center of economics. The characteristic of markets is the decentralization of decision-making. In markets, information flows from one individual to another. According to Adam Smith, the decisive, all-connecting notion of human existence lies in constant exchange with others. This begins with communication and moves via economic exchange to the exchange of values and value judgments that are based on both. Once we realize this, then the requirement to submit to the laws of the market assumes a completely different connotation. We are not submitting to an alien power, but to our own values and rules. At this point it is crucial to consider Adam Smith's *Theory of Moral Sentiments*. This theory provides an essential qualification to the regime of the market. Following Smith, alongside a natural tendency towards self-interest, humans possess an innate capacity for empathy and beneficence towards their fellow human beings. And this is the origin of the behavioral rules and the morality that govern our societies and therefore our economic system. For capitalism to work for the good of all, it must be constrained by the demands of our morality. For Adam Smith, capitalism is not an enclosed system, because the nature of markets depends on the respective cultural conditions, which are influenced by norms and trust. Markets are therefore malleable products of civilization. But capitalism is more than the market. Capitalism is the universalization, that is, the generalization, of the importance of capital. It derives its dynamic from the accumulation of capital. The accumulation of capital alone created something new in history—economic growth. This dynamic becomes very clear during the Industrial Revolution, when capitalism's excesses were all too clearly in evidence, and low wages and the creation of monopolies increasingly fueled economic growth—but at a tremendous human cost. When agriculture dominated economic life, there had been no such momentum. Growth is necessary in a healthy market. Static or even shrinking economies cause people to become cruel and selfish as the battle over resources increases. An economy is like a cosmology: a growing market is like a growing universe.

Each generation of capitalism has always identified different frameworks. In history, capitalism has shown that it can function under a variety of conditions, because it is not tied to a particular organizational system. The only indispensable basis is the constitutional—or at least the law-abiding—state, because only the latter can establish the notion of liability. Ultimately, a system can only achieve reliable and sustainable security through the law. The question that arises here, therefore, is whether capitalism needs democracy, and whether only the latter can reliably safeguard the constitutional state. We have to consider how reliable the rule of law is in non-democratic states.

Today, in light of technological and social developments, many future forms of market economy are conceivable. Some commentators even envisage complete collapse. It is also possible that capitalism might disappear. What can be established with certainty is that capitalism is in transformation. Crises in the financial sector, high public debt, asset prices inflated by a zero-interest rate policy, an unstable banking system (such as in Italy) on the one hand, and, above all, the phenomenon of digitalization, on the other are seen as a threat. We are witnessing a technological revolution. In the near future, we will have an economy driven by artificial intelligence. For example, let's take a closer look at the impact of digitalization on the world of work. There are studies showing that nearly 50 percent of all US jobs are at risk of becoming automated through artificial intelligence over the next ten to twenty years.[1] What impact will such a change in labor markets have on the economy and especially on society? At the moment, people still define themselves through their work. What would happen if this central concept disappears?

Digitalization has given rise to monopolistic mega-corporations, which have for several years been among the biggest players on the stock markets, but whose stock market value does not coincide with their real value. The gap between a company's growth and its value is getting increasingly larger. In a market where digitalization is becoming increasingly prevalent, the classical categories of industrial capitalism no longer apply. The boundaries between employee and employer are becoming blurred. For example, is an Uber driver still an employee or an independent entrepreneur now? While in industrial capitalism it was still clear-cut who ultimately got the profits, in digital capitalism this is often not obvious. In the case of Airbnb, for example, it is primarily the online platform that earns the money, not the individual host or landlord. This, in turn, has repercussions on the tax system of countries that currently still have to incorporate the reality of a digital market economy into their structures. This is proving to be a difficult undertaking.

Digitalization has even broadened what we understand by the term "capital." Data, it is commonly agreed, is the capital of the future. It is therefore essential to pay attention to how this data is distributed and who has ownership of it. Indeed, a concentration of data also results in a concentration of wealth and power. Take, for example, a company such as Facebook. The value of such a company does not lie in its platform, but in the data it has harvested from its users over the years. We live in the age of data, which will also lead to macroeconomic shifts, because successful algorithms based on artificial intelligence work better the more data that is available for analysis. This will be crucial in the upcoming implementation of artificial intelligence and may bring advantages to countries such as China, where the constraints on the harvesting of data are, if anything, even laxer than they are in the West.

Digitalization has also intensified globalization, which simultaneously poses a great challenge and is viewed by many as a threat. From the beginning, capitalism was characterized by a quest for foreign markets. Terrestrial globalization was first undertaken by Christian seafaring and later implemented politically by European colonialism. The term globalization was used for the first time in the 1970s to describe the internationalization of markets. It is characteristic of today's electronic globalization that it encompasses the entire globe, and transcends the territorial boundaries of nation states.[2] The digital networking of the world dissolves the boundaries between markets, regions, companies, machines, and people. The result is mobile, global—but potentially unregulated—business. The world is becoming virtual, and thus offers both the opportunity of transitioning to a unified system of values or to an unchecked monopoly capitalism and an ever greater proliferation of the Internet's potential for the malign as well as for the good.

Globalization has simplified and promoted the movement of people, cultures, technologies, and ideas. This has also contributed to the spread of the capitalist economic system. Now capitalism has turned into capitalisms. Various forms of the capitalist system are emerging—forms that are very different from the Western free market economy, but which are now playing an extremely important role at the global economic level. China is an extremely striking example of this. Formerly referred to as the "workshop of the world" and its businesses ridiculed as copycats, today China is both a serious competitor and an important trading partner for the established Western economies. Its economic strength is evident precisely in its extraordinary economic growth. By switching from a planned economy to a market economy, China has lifted more than 700 million people out of poverty within just a few decades. In 2025, China will probably be one of the world's high-income countries.[3] The capitalism China is currently experiencing is clearly different from Western capitalism. China has found a way of creating a capitalist system in which the state has a significant influence on markets. It is still unclear how the global market will react as a result of geopolitical shifts. A rivalry between the US and China is already starkly in evidence. A change of consciousness can be observed, to the extent that rivalry and a series of adversarial relations is replacing the former hoped-for integration that characterized the early years of Internet growth. In turn, this struggle is taking place in the field of cutting-edge technologies. Our world and especially the market economy are facing challenges. Since the market is ultimately a product of our civilization—that is, it is shaped by our values and ideas—concepts and visions are needed now more than ever before.

One of the main criticisms of today's capitalism is that we see an ever-increasing inequality between wealth and income. Here the question arises whether it is a phenomenon of modern capitalism that inequality increases within countries. According to critics, capitalism is vulnerable to crisis, is a system that becomes detached from the reality of people's lives, and relies too much on the individual to the detriment of the community. Adam Smith, however, originally saw capitalism as the exact opposite, namely as the opportunity of creating collective prosperity through individual efforts. For although capitalism is based above all on the concept of the individual, its configurations have an effect on the coexistence of us all. Capitalism must serve the common good, the *bonum commune*, the general well-being of a society.

Since the essence of capitalism entails constant effort and a perpetual will for more, our world is doing considerably better, in many respects, today than it did just 30 years ago.[4] The free market economy has contributed much to the increasing prosperity of humanity—and so the individualistic character of capitalism has in fact proved profitable for general prosperity.

But for Adam Smith's basic idea to remain relevant to the capitalism of the future, our economic system needs care and attention. It is therefore essential to ask questions about the future of capitalism. How should capitalism be interpreted today so that our values and ideals are not torpedoed but supported?

This volume looks at capitalism's future from different perspectives and tries to find possible creative approaches to the current challenges. The aim is not to abandon the current economic system in its entirety, but to look forward constructively and critically and thus to shape the future not only of our economy but of our society as well.

Corinne Michaela Flick, January 2019

Notes

1. Cf. for example the study by Carl Benedikt Frey and Michael Osborne, "The Future of Employment: How Susceptible Are Jobs to Computerisation?" in *Technological Forecasting and Social Change*, 114 (2016), pp. 254–280. https://doi.org/10.1016/j.techfore.2016.08.019 (accessed on 08.10.2018). See also the Convoco interview with Carl Benedikt Frey, "The Future of Employment" in Corinne Michaela Flick (ed.), *The Common Good in the 21st Century* (Munich: Convoco! Editions, 2018).

2. Cf. Peter Sloterdijk, *In the World Interior of Capital* (Cambridge: Polity, 2013), pp. 27 ff.

3. Cf. Justin Yifu Lin in this volume and in his book *The Quest for Prosperity: How Developing Economies Can Take Off* (Princeton, NJ: Princeton University Press, 2012).

4. Cf. Branko Milanovic and Christoph Lakner, "Global Income Distribution: From the Fall of the Berlin Wall to the Great Recession" in *World Bank Economic Review* 2015, pp. 203–217. https://doi.org/10.1093/wber/lhv039 (accessed on 05.11.2018).

THESES

LUCIO BACCARO

Growth is a very important political goal for governments, since it facilitates reelection and assuages distributive conflict. However, there is no single blueprint for growth, but different "growth models." Growth models, in turn, rest on "dominant social blocs," which produce a legitimating discourse, i.e. they are able to present the interests of the bloc as coinciding with the national interest.

CORINNE M. FLICK

Today, in light of technological and social developments, many future forms of market economy are conceivable. Some commentators even envisage complete collapse. It is also possible that capitalism might disappear. What can be established with certainty is that capitalism is in transformation.

ALBRECHT RITSCHL

Until the Middle Ages, religious and institutional barriers presented an impediment to the emergence of capitalism by means of a separation between invested and risk capital. Medieval Italian trading companies were a first step towards overcoming these obstacles, while in the Netherlands the development of markets for limited liability share capital created the breakthrough. From the very beginning, capitalist methods of finance have been associated with seafaring and globalization, and equally financial crises have been crises of globalization.

KAI A. KONRAD

The market-based economic system with private property has brought unprecedented prosperity to very broad strata of the population in Europe. Industry 4.0 (the fourth industrial revolution) might continue this development. However, for this to happen society must be open to progress and change. If European societies are not prepared to do so and block these changes, prosperity will be created elsewhere in future.

STEFAN KORIOTH

The relationship between the market and democracy is ambivalent. Economic and political freedom can be mutually supportive. However, free markets can also undermine the willingness to engage in fair, collective cooperation in the interests of the common good. In principle, economic freedom can also be protected by authoritarian regimes. The only question is whether this can succeed in the long run.

STEFAN OSCHMANN

The future of capitalism will largely be defined in the People's Republic of China. This is not entirely without irony given that the ruling Communist Party is officially committed to Marxism and the "socialist market economy."

JUSTIN YIFU LIN

The secret of China's success is her use of both the "invisible hand" and "visible hand," forming an organic integration, complementation, and mutual improvement of the functions of the market and the state.

MONIKA SCHNITZER

Without a political voice, it is hard to imagine that legal certainty can be guaranteed. Equally, a state that the people no longer trust to act in their interests will pay for this with a decline in economic momentum.

WOLFGANG SCHÖN

Digitalization is accelerating tax competition. The high mobility of intangible assets and the decreasing importance of real investment and labor mean that corporation taxes are decreasing while sales taxes are increasing. This calls into question the fundamental ability of tax systems to create equality in society. It remains doubtful whether this trend can be counteracted by stepping up income taxes, property taxes, or inheritance taxes.

RUDOLF MELLINGHOFF

Free economic activity as one of the basic requirements of capitalism can only develop if the state provides the conditions that allow an exchange of goods and services, if it ensures a financial market and a functioning banking system, and if legal rights are guaranteed by the state and, if possible, enforced through independent courts. The tax state thus proves to be the ideal state form in which a free-market economy can develop.

CHRISTOPH G. PAULUS

Capitalism's transformation can also be seen in the way that artificial intelligence is making entire professions disappear and cutting off armies of citizens from work and income opportunities. Equally, this is a massive threat to democracy. What may help with regard to this scenario is the unconditional investment in education. Knowledge and education for all must become the universal program of European politics.

TIMO MEYNHARDT

The element of the abstract, that which is detached from an immediate emotional relationship, was originally a great advance in terms of freedom and an engine of progress. However, the phenomena of our current crisis demonstrate that the old balance between the concrete (community) and the abstract (society) has been lost.

ADAM CURTIS

What Adam Smith said right at the beginning about the whole idea of morals is central to his idea of capitalism. It's not just about the market. It's about you having the capacity and wanting to think about how other people feel and how possibly you could make them feel better. And maybe that is what is coming, and that is maybe what is going to rescue capitalism.

SEAN HAGAN

If we place exclusive reliance on regulations and rules in the fight against corruption, we will simply invite circumvention. What we need is not a culture of compliance but a culture of values. Indeed, we need to have public officials and private actors who do the right thing even though no one is watching.

HERBERT A. REITSAMER

The brain's reward mechanism makes us pursue prosperity and accumulate riches. We can see greed for more as a relic of our phylogenetic development and as the burden or blessing of evolution. However, it must be clear to us in all our actions that, in a certain sense, we humans still act using our frog brain and that primitive, neuronal control circuits influence our decisions.

BAZON BROCK

In their very assertion that they are based on economic data, the concepts traditionally used to celebrate or critique capitalism overlook the most important fact that it is above all counterfactuals that matter in society. The most significant fact is that all societies are subject to the normativity of the counterfactual.

HANS ULRICH OBRIST

The involvement of artists at the center of society is extremely interesting when we talk about the future—the future not only of art but of society. Every company, every ministry, every corporation should have an artist-in-residence.

JÖRG ROCHOLL

Growth is not a decision variable, but rather a target variable. It is produced by creativity, mutually beneficial trade, and work—that is through human endeavors. Arbitrary interventions, as demanded by radical growth critics, represent a huge infringement of freedom and could quickly lead to an authoritarian system.

GISBERT RÜHL

Now a public issue, platform capitalism describes a new digital economic system, namely an enhanced form of capitalism. Capitalism is essentially defined as "private ownership of the means of production." In the age of platform capitalism, this relationship is in part dissolved: private ownership of information becomes the constituent principle of platform capitalism.

JENS BECKERT

The future of scientific and economic development should more fully reflect their consequences for the political community and for society as a whole. Where do we really want to go?

CHAPTER 1

A HISTORICAL PERSPECTIVE ON CAPITALISM AND ITS CRITIQUE

ALBRECHT RITSCHL

INTRODUCTION

What is capitalism, historically speaking? In what way does it differ from earlier economic forms, and why did it arise in the first place? Was the new system based on innovation, something new that had not occurred to the ancients? Or was it made possible by the abolition of restrictions? Did it unleash forces that had previously not been allowed to develop? And did this new phenomenon, whatever the cause of its unfettering, have its origins in entrepreneurship or in finance?

Early forms of capitalism existed since the birth of the great agricultural and urban cultures in the Middle East and China. Wherever agricultural surpluses were skimmed off on a large scale to feed urban populations, commercial agricultural operations were required. Extensive irrigation projects, urban development, and the associated infrastructure, temple complexes, a priesthood, standing armies, and last but not least long-distance trade, all had to be paid for. All this presupposed, in addition to taxation, at any rate a rudimentary system of credit, not least because of the periodic nature of the harvesting cycle. Despite their achievements, however, it would be wrong to call these early civilizations capitalist. Of course, there was no lack of merchants and occasional mergers in merchant companies, in the case of overseas trading companies, for example. However, it is clear that major projects were often controlled by the authorities, as the Old Testament describes in the case of Egypt and the precautions it took against drought. In addition, there is evidence that regulations concerning credit transactions already existed in antiquity.

In Ancient Mesopotamia, under the Code of Hammurabi[1] it was initially permitted to charge interest on loans, albeit with an upper limit. Later on, however, the relevant regulations were deleted from the legal code. The Old Testament tells of a ban on calculating interest on debts ["usury"] between members of the tribes of Israel, but not on people outside the tribes.[2] In addition, there were limitations on the duration of contractual obligations, which are similar in parts to the Code of Hammurabi.

NO CAPITALISM IN THE ROMAN EMPIRE

Ancient Greece and Rome placed hardly any restrictions on entrepreneurship, albeit only as far as free citizens were concerned; and there is evidence of a rudimentary banking system involving deposit and checking trans-actions. However, as everywhere in antiquity, these were essentially the activities of individual traders who, like the moneychangers in the temple described in the New Testament, more or less specialized in financial transactions.[3] Diocletian's reforms imposed significant restrictions on the freedom of trade in antiquity and a—failed—regulation to freeze prices, which foreshadowed the transition to medieval guilds and their rigid rules.

But what about capitalism in the heyday of the Roman Empire? We have to ask why modern capitalism did not emerge at that time, as the conditions of production that could produce a more modern kind of economy were certainly not lacking. In the Roman Empire, agricultural productivity, an important indicator of the preconditions for transitioning to modern economic growth, was at a level that would not be reached again until the 18th century. In the areas of road maintenance and water supply, the Roman Empire produced achievements which only the 19th century would approach: the military roads crisscrossing the whole of southern and western Europe were the freeways of the Roman Empire, as it were, and the long-term effects of Roman urban planning can still be seen in the layout of West European cities.

On the other hand, it can be argued that Ancient Rome, and even more so the Hellenic world, contained the technical, but perhaps not the institutional conditions for sustained growth, as both were slave-owning societies. Why modernize and increase productivity when slave labor was available at minimum cost? The fact that slavery can be a serious obstacle to the transition to a modernized economy has been discussed intensively and controversially using the example of the southern states of America before the Civil War. Nevertheless, when the Roman Empire stopped expanding around 150 CE, the influx of slaves seems to have slowed, and the institution itself appears to have become less important. In addition, with the proliferation of cheap food from the provinces, unemployment in Rome and neighboring areas grew, and more and more Italian farms were abandoned. This freeing-up of agricultural labor, however, is a precondition for the transition to modern growth with its structural, sectoral change away from agriculture. Moreover, Italy, as the heartland of the Roman Empire, enjoyed considerable tax privileges. So if not here, where else could the transition to a capitalist, profit-oriented economy have succeeded?

THREE REFORMS IN MEDIEVAL ITALY

This still unexplained paradox is all the more important, as Italy was the region where, a thousand years later, those very changes took place which had failed to appear in the Roman Empire, and gradually spread from there. In the medieval Italian city-states, three developments emerged almost simultaneously that have given modern capitalism its character: a commercial manufacturing industry, the financing of loans through bills of exchange, and the development of the legal form of the firm.

In his dissertation, Max Weber compared the Italian legal form of the "firm" with older legal forms, such as the *commenda*, which were widely used in maritime financing and could be traced back to antiquity, and the *societas* of Roman law—but found no direct precursors.[4] The new feature of the firm was that it had both full and limited liability partners, a model that had not previously existed other than in the limited-time shipping companies of the *commenda*. Even Roman law and its business practice seem not to have included this distinction. There were, of course, associations that took on public contracts as consortia, but the *socii* had unlimited liability, similar to today's civil law partnership [*Gesellschaft bürgerlichen Rechts*], which was modeled on such associations.[5]

The new institution of the firm proved to be a success in accumulating capital and growing businesses. Larger factories and trading companies could now be run as family businesses, for example, without each investor being at the same time a personally liable member of the management, as the partnership model of the Roman *societas* suggested, or the company being liquidated after every expedition when it had fulfilled its limited business objective, as in the case of the *commenda*. It is still surprising that the *commenda* did not adopt a more enduring form as a permanent company. Weber argues in great detail that the firm had its roots instead in the Lombard Laws concerning joint inheritance and family foundations, which were created to ensure the survival of the patrimony without burdening all family members with liability.

The second institutional innovation of the Italian Middle Ages was the establishment of cashless payment and credit transactions, based on the bill of exchange. An important factor in this was the circumvention of religious observations. In an early version of the critique of capitalism, Church scholars argued that collecting interest on repayment of a loan seemed like doubling the burden of the credit, because unlike livestock or crops, money did not reproduce of its own accord. Church doctrine did not oppose companies making profits that were derived from the reproduction of commodities. The ban was directed against a fixed interest rate, which placed the income of the debtor alone at risk. There were many reasons for such a ban, in particular the plight of the borrower, who could be left without income through no fault of their own. Old Testament provisions for the limitation of debt bondage and periodic debt relief were already in use to protect them. On the other hand, the ban on interest must have been a stumbling block to investment, because any kind of risk-sharing between the investor and the entrepreneur as a contribution towards profit-sharing requires business results that are clearly visible to both parties. In the case of shipping loans under the *commenda*, precise procedural rules ensured that expedition proceeds were recorded by impartial observers. In an ongoing business with changing projects, on the other hand, a sophisticated accounting system was needed, which developed and gradually expanded as the firm spread throughout Italy. Without the aid of such complex mechanisms, the individual merchant relied on surpluses from previous ventures or, at best, on silent capital contributions that were based on trust and depended for their enforceability on returns expected from a continuing mutual business relationship. Alternatively, there were the Jewish moneylenders, who assumed complex financial transactions from early on.

The new element introduced by the bill of exchange was first of all the circumvention of the ban on interest through the use of exchange fees. This was justified by the exchange rate risk incurred when making transfers to foreign financial centers. In its design, the bill of exchange was a fee-based transfer, later usually made by the recipient or an intermediary bank as an advance on the transport of goods. The exchange fee was justified by the exchange rate risk incurred when making transactions to external locations. At the destination, the bills were periodically cleared against other bills drawn at the departure location and the clearing credits compensated for or carried forward in the form of new bills to the next financial period. Italy, and subsequently the whole of Europe, soon developed a method of cross-border cashless payment, later followed by the establishment of regional clearing fairs, often on the sidelines of regular trade fairs. Clearing and collective exchange assumed derivative functions. Well before this, people had discovered that the bill could be used for pure credit transactions, in direct opposition to Church regulations. The only requirement was a transfer from A to B and a return bill of exchange (*recambium*) from B to A. The credit period corresponded to the duration of the respective bills: about two months between Western and Southern Europe; six weeks within the Mediterranean region. There is also evidence for the existence of bills that were drawn on issuers in other places and were apparently disputed. During the dual time-period until the bill returned to its place of issue and the original payment transaction was reversed, credit had come into effect, and the transfer was made only for appearance's sake. For the religious authorities, such transactions could not be monitored to any extent, and indeed were difficult to comprehend. As a result, the bill of exchange became a universal, increasingly tradable instrument of payment and credit, and a class of Catholic bankers and traders operating across Europe, known as Lombards, came into being.[6]

Increasingly, this system became linked with a rejection of earlier traditions. In place of the independent trader, the firm emerged, grew in size, and expanded its activities internationally in trading, finance, and production, resulting in large global firms such as the Augsburg trading houses of the Fuggers and the Welsers. Their often decentralized organization made them well-suited to Europe's political fragmentation into numerous micro-territories, but also played a key role in the major expeditions that were opening up the maritime routes and the Latin American colonies. But this is precisely what sealed the fate of capitalism's first flourishing. The rapid growth in the Spanish Habsburgs' power placed these companies in the grip of a capital-hungry sovereign who dragged them down into the maelstrom of a series of state bankruptcies, thus bringing their heyday to an end.

PROPERTY RIGHTS AND THE RISE OF
CAPITALISM

With the discovery of the maritime routes to India and the New World, however, Europe's economic focus shifted to the sea-faring nations along the Atlantic coast. Of particular importance for this further development were the Netherlands, who had won their independence from the Spanish Habsburgs over the course of long wars and who gave rise to one particular development. A feature of the 17th-century Dutch Golden Age was a certain degree of religious tolerance, which made the Netherlands a haven for victims of religious persecution, especially Portuguese Jews. Also, innovative methods of capital accumulation were emerging in the Netherlands. The newly formed United East India Company (VOC), with its state monopoly, issued shares traded on the Amsterdam stock exchange. Exchange trading had existed since the Renaissance in numerous European settings, including Augsburg and Nuremberg, but mostly in the trading of currencies and debt securities. Trading in company shares, especially mining, had existed since the Middle Ages, but shareholders risked being liable for additional payments—an obligation to make supplementary payments should the company make a loss. The Dutch innovation was to list prominent companies on the stock exchange with freely tradable share certificates, whose liability was limited to the purchase price—contrary to what had initially applied to England's East India Company of the same era.

Now, the VOC was not an example of free-market entrepreneurship as it was a quasi-state monopoly whose profits were largely based on the exercise of military power. But the separation of the management from the shareholders was now complete, and a step had been taken towards valuation by the capital market. This system was able to flourish under the laws of the Dutch Republic, which gave the merchant class a stake in political power and thus the government budget. More particularly, the activities of the VOC were separate from those of the general public budget, so that the transfer of capital was not in itself a form of indirect public-sector finance, unlike the Habsburg expeditions financed by the Fuggers and the Welsers. The preconditions for the success of these innovations were on the one hand the establishment of inalienable property rights that created and underpinned confidence in the new institutions, and on the other the absence of a sovereign who was independent of the people and whose financial problems could jeopardize the legal system. The former was largely guaranteed in the Netherlands, while the status of the then so-called *stadtholder* was a source of ongoing conflict.

A similar development occurred in England following the end of the Civil War with the Glorious Revolution of 1688, which was itself a revolutionary import from the Netherlands and which concluded with the then *stadtholder* being crowned English king. To secure his election, the new monarch granted the Bill of Rights, which granted Parliament far-reaching rights regarding tax, borrowing, and the declaration of war. In 1694, to obtain war loans against France, the monarch supported the founding of the Bank of England, which gave the merchant class even more control over the government budget. In these financial innovations of the early British and Dutch colonial eras, we can see all the essential features of a capitalist economy that is largely driven by investment capital.[7]

There is, however, one reservation. In both countries, 18th-century trading capitalism may have delayed industrialization rather than acting as its driver. And the desired stabilization of financial markets and public finances did not occur in the first instance—rather the opposite. Investors' speculation focused on exotic agricultural products, such as the Dutch tulip mania of the late 17th century, or on more licenses to exploit colonial areas such as during the South Sea Bubble in London and, at the same time, the Mississippi Bubble in Paris between 1719 and 1721. The South Sea Company had a monopoly of England's trade with the Spanish colonies in Latin America, which, however, yielded only modest returns. The real aim of their business was to assume elements of Britain's war debt. Disinformation about the business outlook had stimulated the sale of shares. The feeling of euphoria soon led to huge price increases, followed by an equally sharp downturn. As a result, several members of the government were sacked, and the Chancellor of the Exchequer went to jail for fraud. A similar scheme in France gave the Compagnie d'Occident a trading monopoly of French possessions in North America, which were still at that time the entire Midwest of the later United States and large parts of Canada. As in England, this scheme aimed to pay off public debt, and government bonds could be exchanged for shares in the Compagnie. Soon, the scheme became too successful, more government bonds and banknotes were issued and used to speculate on the rapidly rising shares of the company. The result was inflation and sovereign bankruptcy.[8]

In both cases, commercial enterprises ostensibly served public finance and were no better than the model of tax-farming, whereby the financially threatened Habsburgs sold tax or customs revenues or the proceeds from gold and silver mines to finance their debt. The collapsing prices following this wave of speculation are the classical phenomena of stock-market crashes. It is, however, important to note in this case that these were exotic securities with no intrinsic value for the development of the public economy, not bread-and-butter stocks whose issuance finances real investment. Thus there is credible evidence that the high borrowing requirements for first the Dutch then the English naval wars prevented investment capital from being put to more productive use. England's industrialization began with the technical innovations of the 18th century in coal, steel, and textile machinery, but only gained momentum in the 19th century. The Netherlands, however, did not industrialize at all at first, but were only gripped by modernization during the second wave of the Industrial Revolution that was driven by electrical engineering. The same applies to the once proud trading cities of Italy, which began to sink into insignificance from the 18th century onwards, and which impress today's visitors with their museum-like beauty rather than their vibrant economic life.

The lessons of the 18th century have been of crucial importance for the liberal understanding of capitalism in classical economics. State activity had to be confined to public security and order, monarchs' crazy spending was to be tightly constrained by political scrutiny as far as possible, the stimulation of the economy through public debt was denounced as illusory with higher taxation the inevitable result—and the outcome was that both instruments of state finance ultimately amounted to the same thing. And the newly awakened interest in public limited companies had been delivered a significant setback. The incentive problems of the management, which overruled the interests of shareholders, seemed too big. In future, the instrument of the public limited company was only to be used for infrastructure projects without particular entrepreneurial challenges. Under the influence of these lessons, the stock market in Germany, for example, remained heavily regulated until the 1860s.

THE INDUSTRIAL REVOLUTION

In the 19th century, the conception of capitalism and its critique were strongly influenced by the social side effects of industrialization. Although Karl Marx himself did not highlight industrialization as such, he included it in a wide-reaching panorama. However, his fixation on the physical production of commodities narrowed

the subject considerably—and certainly inappropri-
ately. Friedrich Engels' social critique of conditions in
working-class slums in England's industrial regions did
the rest. It was easy to add descriptions of the miser-
able lot of Silesian weavers and—with some hesita-
tion regarding England—the wretchedness of workers
under German industrialization. As a theorist, Marx
was not really original in his approach, as his theories can be seamlessly integrated into the pessimistic,
classical economics of the early 19th century. This had
begun with Robert Malthus's population theories, and
emerged fully formed in David Ricardo's speculations
on the surplus value of mechanized production. Marx's
innovation was to connect these theories with a wide-
ranging philosophy of history. But even these classical
British economists, like Marx later on, predicted capitalism's lack of sustainability as an economic system
that was designed to permanently increase general
prosperity but could not manage it. All these gloomy
prophecies depended on a new phenomenon of the
late 18th century: the incipient decline in mortality
alongside continually high birth rates, which led to the
creation of an unemployed, chronically undernour-
ished "industrial reserve army." Later, this pattern
would be repeated frequently; it was the beginning of
the global population explosion. From the mid-19th

century, however, overall birth rates began to decline in Northwestern Europe, and gradually production growth and technological progress translated into a rising standard of living for the general population, which the pessimists of the early 19th century, later followed by Marx, had not expected.

Britain's industrialization was atypical for the previous pattern in terms of its finance which, unlike the great colonial ventures of the 17th and 18th centuries, at first bypassed the established capital markets. The new boom in mining and steel, with their downstream industries such as engineering and later railroad construction, seems to have been financed like a gold rush outside London to begin with, driven by the great profits made through the new opportunities for using coal in iron smelting. The major financial centers were increasingly used to finance industrial exports, i.e. in their traditional overseas trade. In the mid-19th century, England exported entire railroad systems throughout the world on a turnkey basis, including technicians and maintenance personnel. The first German railroad line from Nuremberg to Fürth is a (rather small) example of such an export.

In the context of these wide-ranging capital exports, the first international credit crises, most of them originating from the US, soon emerged—crises that have played a major role in the critique of capitalism ever since. This was due to the enormous amount of capital required for the opening-up of transport connections, especially in North America, which was largely promoted by British equipment and financed from London. As we have seen, financing overseas ventures was nothing new, and dated back to the 15th century. Even the financial crisis of 1720–21 had been linked to it—but at that time still as speculation on the future. The novelty, however, was that financial crises now occurred frequently and irregularly, caused by a changing mixture of great expectations that were then disappointed, fluctuating land prices, and recurrent shortages of international capital. The relations of industrial production in capital goods, which were Marx's focus, probably had the least to do with the calamity in question. The decisive factor in the rapid development of infrastructure in America and later elsewhere in the New World was rapidly changing conditions and local forecasts of the future.

THE EUROPEAN RESPONSE: ORGANIZED
CAPITALISM

The industrialization of Europe did not, in general, follow the English model. In Europe, industry was initially self-financing, as it were, so a lack of capital on the continent was considered a serious problem. At first, the idea of developing industries locally seemed more expensive than importing from England, and so apart from the German Customs Union's mild protective tariff, later strengthened by Bismarck's customs legislation, industrialization and its finance became the subject of political attention. Unlike in England, the instrument used was a banking system, which carried all banking activities at the same time, thus serving as a hub for capital accumulation and focus on the industries of the future. Licensed by the state, such all-purpose banks were set up in France, Belgium, and Germany, and were devoted to the politically desirable task of skimming off private savings from a rapidly growing network of regional capital depositories and directing the surpluses into loans for industry.

Soon the industrial and political functions for managing these new financial institutions could no longer be ignored—an issue for which the critique of capitalism invented the term "organized capitalism":

organized by the private sector, but in coordination with government policy and often on government initiative. Of course, such a fusion of public policy and private interest was not new in any way; the innovation lay in the generalization of this system.[9]

This system transition too was accompanied by crisis. The liberalization of stock-market law in Germany in the second half of the 19th century initially led to a wave of new public limited companies. Like today, these "start-ups" geared their activities towards new technologies—at that time mechanical engineering in particular. As in the current boom of start-ups, the *Gründerzeit* also produced its own crash, the *Gründerkrise* crisis of 1873. Like today, the newly founded companies of the time had been financed using venture capital, albeit largely via share issues on the regular stock exchange. The *Gründerkrach* crash, with its impressive crop of non-viable start-ups has had far-reaching consequences for the reputation of the capital market among the German public. It became fashionable to distrust the stock market and to entrust one's savings to the bank in supposed security, or to invest in government securities, fueled by growing public debt.

Capitalism now came in for criticism from both left and right. On the left, the new system of what was now called "finance capitalism" appeared to be another attempt to escape the gloomy prophecies of Marx and others of a downward trend in the rate of profit. According to this new trend, capitalist dynamics did not derive from heavy industry, as Marx and the classic British economists claimed, but from the banks and their control of industrial interests.[10] On the right, the system was criticized using similar arguments: their propaganda against unfettered capitalism was laced with shrill, anti-Semitic overtones. In the German Reich, the stock market was subject to constraints, trade using derivatives was severely limited, and industrial finance became even more heavily reliant than before on loans from the big banks. On the eve of World War I, in Germany in particular, capitalism encountered a crisis of legitimacy, despite the first signs of prosperity, which were gradually spreading to other sections of the population.

Between the World Wars, this problem grew into the most serious crisis capitalism had faced so far. World War I left behind not only destruction and shattered public finances, but also a working class in turmoil; following the example of Russia, revolutions appeared to be imminent and were only suppressed with difficulty, as in Germany. In the postwar period of inflation, the middle class of white-collar workers and officials who had turned away from the stock market lost their savings. International relations were poisoned by demands for reparations, as collection of the full amount remained illusory; this initially diverted international cash flows which then dried up completely. America closed its doors to further mass immigration, turning away from the liberal policies of the 19th century. As a result of all these upheavals, global industrial production collapsed by one-third after 1929— a hitherto unprecedented disaster in the history of the previous two hundred years. Which of these individual factors ultimately triggered this collapse remains controversial and may ultimately be a futile question; in a systemic breakdown of such magnitude, the simultaneous failure of several parts of the system must be involved, and each individual factor alone would have been enough to cause a mid-sized financial crisis.

AFTER THE SYSTEMIC CRISIS: STATE INTERVENTION AND CONTROL OF THE CAPITAL MARKETS

The politics of the 1930s sought a way out of this systemic crisis in mutual economic isolation and the return to wartime, economic planning that seemed to have enjoyed success not least in the Soviet Union. The predominant feature was the extensive suppression of international capital movements on both sides of the Atlantic. In relation to its neighbors, Germany took this system to extremes with a tight network of capital and foreign-exchange controls. Capitalism was increasingly replaced by state capital controls, which if required used private legal structures as a disguise, but actually used the resources to fund political and military priorities.

During World War II, this command economy led to considerable increases in production on all sides, but also to enormous investments in war-related, heavy industries, which later on, when reconstruction and the economic miracle tailed off, lay idle due to overcapacity, and were dismantled in a painful process of adjustment. It was only at the end of 2018 that coal production in Germany ceased, although the economic need for an exit from coal production in the future had already been recognized during the interwar period. This repeated shift was initially due to the wartime policy of economic self-sufficiency. After a brief period of recovery in reconstruction, the transition began in the coal crisis of 1958, but was delayed again and again to cushion the social impact with high subsidies—over a period of 60 years nevertheless.

In the postwar period, capital market and international capital controls persisted, albeit to a lesser extent. The prevailing model was mixed economies with a high proportion of public or government-led investment. West Germany was no exception. Numerous government investment and subsidy programs ranging from housing construction to the oil industry have had a significant impact on the Federal Republic of Germany. With the currency reform of 1948, state control of the private sector was lifted in many areas, unlike in England or France, for example. However, the privatization of state industries established under the Third Reich dragged on until the 1970s, and even longer in the coal industry. For a long time, artificially low interest rates coupled with rationed access to loans were among the consequences of these state interventions, as were serious shortfalls in the market values of large German companies due to their stock market capitalization. When a centralized universal banking system was re-established in the mid-1950s, the major banks once again resumed their traditional role of serving as a hub for corporate lending and investment decisions and of exercising significant influence on recruitment at board level.

In these clearly interventionist models, critiques of capitalism could only come from the left, in particular the trade union movement, which sought to participate in corporate management. It is not without a certain irony that this was more successful in West Germany than in neighboring Western European countries, but it fits with the tradition of corporatism as an artificial community of capital and labor, which had already inspired the creation of social security in Germany and resonated deeply within the conservative political camp. At the same time, Britain's attempt to involve the trade union movement directly in political power led to the Labour Party losing power, and to a massive strike movement in reaction to the regulatory about-turn imposed by Prime Ministers Heath and Thatcher.

THE MARKET ECONOMY'S CRITIQUE OF STATE INTERVENTIONISM

However, this turnaround was anticipated by another critique of capitalism that branded the existing system of state interventionism as a kind of insidious socialism and the enemy of freedom. Since the interwar period, this critique had been promulgated by the Austrian School, especially Ludwig von Mises[11] and the young Friedrich von Hayek.[12] In more moderate form, the same critique also underpinned the German economic logic of Walter Eucken and others, who had offered a contemporary critique of the Third Reich's wartime economic planning as a centralized economy, and had even found a degree of support within the regime.[13] In the postwar era, this critique could be applied to the malfunctioning of state-managed capitalism, and with good reason. This gradual about-turn has been supported by recent work on the functioning of markets as a mechanism for coordinating information,[14] which suggested the exact opposite of the policy of restricting capital markets at that time.

This political sea change can be traced back to around 1980, following the collapse of the Bretton Woods monetary system and subsequent international adjustment inflation, which could not be controlled by the interventionist policies being applied until that time. Under the influence of the new doctrines, a fierce policy to combat inflation now began, accompanied by a wave of privatization in the public sector. At the same time, a new paradigm emerged for tackling the debt crises that had hit Latin America and other emerging economies in the 1970s. Soon this new formula was referred to as the "Washington Consensus," which consisted of a combination of cautious fiscal policy alongside tax reforms, privatization, the deregulation of international markets, and the liberalization of international capital movements.[15]

However, it would be too easy to attribute the subsequent accelerated integration of the world economy, which was soon criticized as globalization, solely to these changes in policy. It is true that the new political paradigm brought an international harmonization of national economic policy that was in retrospect astonishing. Debt relief for countries in what used to be called the Third World took the edge off the growing critique of globalization. Above all, this was happening in the face of an undeniable increase in prosperity that could not be explained by the Marxist doctrines espoused by some critics.

THE COLLAPSE OF COMMUNISM AND ITS CONSEQUENCES

However, these trends took place against the backdrop of the major turning point created by the international collapse of Communism. Within a short period of time, from eastern Central Europe to China, a huge workforce emerged, looking for profitable employment, and this was combined with a shortage of capital to equip this workforce with the necessary capital goods and technologies. As a result of this turnaround in the scarcity of labor, wages came under pressure internationally and capital returns increased. Eastern Europe and East Asia quickly became the extended workshop of the developed economies, destabilizing the hard-won political balance between labor and capital in the Western world. Adaptation to this shift has still not been accomplished: it has spawned a new class of those left behind by globalization in the form of workers in traditional industries in the West, and has sparked a new wave of the critique of capitalism. In some respect, this critique mirrors the Washington Consensus.[16] Neither the countries of East Asia nor India seem to have followed its formulae for a policy of market deregulation; and instead political management, a mix of public and private enterprise, and a policy of targeted protective tariffs dominate.[17] In short, East Asia's policy of development seems to be a copy of Continental Europe's response to Britain's Industrial Revolution in the 19th century—organized capitalism with sometimes more, sometimes less emphasis on governance through the banking system.[18] The developed world's reaction to this challenge is still a primary target for criticism, however. Today, this critique comes especially from nationalistic positions. As in the 1930s, they regard the remedy once again as cutting-off state economies from global competition. And as then, today too there are complaints that the losers in the globalization process have not been adequately compensated or even that the success of international, especially Chinese, competition is fuelled by totally unfair practices.[19] But unlike in the interwar period, increased competition in world markets is not the result of an acute crisis, but of a long-term structural change that cannot be reversed.

For the first time in the 19th century, the European developed nations experienced the center of world economic development moving away from Europe, and the dynamics of capitalism now being driven by the New World, especially America. At the start of the 21st century, we are experiencing a similar shift in focus. With the rise of China, East Asia's leading position has been shored up for the foreseeable future. The Western world as a whole now faces the same challenge faced by Europe in the early 20th century, namely, coming to terms with a relative loss of importance and the economic burdens of adjusting to the new situation, without succumbing to the siren calls of economic and political extremism.

OUTLOOK

What's next? As we know, predictions are difficult—particularly when they concern the future.
Nevertheless, we can identify some trends. East Asia's
major project of catch-up has slowed significantly in
recent years, as Western levels of income and productivity in its developed regions have been reached. There
are signs that, as in the case of Japan, the production
apparatus has in some places been extended further
than is conducive to maintaining a long-term position in the global market. There is no way that the
high growth rates of the past can be projected into
the future. On the contrary, the slowdown in growth
indicates a swing towards normal or even below-
average rates within the next decade. Conversely, the
economies of North America and parts of Europe have
recovered from the major financial crisis post 2008, to
the extent it is no longer underemployment but low
income levels that are the most pressing issue. In the
medium term, we can expect that with rising wages
in East Asia, cost advantages by comparison with
the West will decrease, and so a return to moderate
wage growth is also possible in the West. As part of
a gradual, global economic modernization, the hitherto above-average growth in corporate profits will

also revert and approach historically normal levels once more. The condition for all these developments, however, is that the coming years remain free of serious political or even military upheavals.

Notes

1. Code of Hammurabi, 88, 89.

2. Deut. 23:20.

3. Matt. 21:12 describes "all them that sold and bought in the temple," "moneychangers," and "them that sold doves"; while John 2:14 writes of "them that sold oxen and sheep" as well as "the changers of money."

4. Max Weber, *The History of Commercial Partnerships in the Middle Ages*, trans. with an introduction by Lutz Kaelber (Lanham, MD: Rowman and Littlefield Publishers, Inc., 2003).

5. See the in-depth description of these long debates in Andreas Fleckner, *Antike Kapitalvereinigungen* (Cologne: Böhlau Verlag, 2010).

6. Fleckner, *Antike Kapitalvereinigungen.*

7. Douglass C. North and Robert Paul Thomas, *The Rise of the Western World. A New Economic History* (Cambridge: Cambridge University Press, 1971).

8. Peter M. Garber, *Famous First Bubbles: The Fundamentals of Early Manias* (Cambridge, MA: The MIT Press, 2000).

9. For an overview see Heinrich August Winkler (ed.), *Organisierter Kapitalismus* (Göttingen: Vandenhoeck & Ruprecht, 1974).

10. Cf. Rudolf Hilferding, *Das Finanzkapital* (Vienna: Wiener Volksbuchhandlung, 1910).

11. Ludwig von Mises, *Kritik Des Interventionismus: Untersuchungen zur Wirtschaftspolitik und Wirtschaftsideologie der Gegenwart* (Jena, 1929).

12. Friedrich A. Hayek, *The Road to Serfdom* (London: Routledge & Sons, 1944).

13. Walter Eucken, *Die Grundlagen der Nationalökonomie* (Jena, 1939).

14. Beginning with Friedrich A. Hayek, "The Use of Knowledge in Society" in *American Economic Review* 35 (1945). On the role of capital markets in the aggregation of information, with a summary of earlier work on the subject, cf. Eugene Fama, *Foundations of Finance* (New York: Basic Books, Inc, 1976).

15. John Williamson, "What Washington Means by Policy Reform" in John Williamson (ed.), *Latin American Adjustment: How Much Has Happened?*, Washington, DC: Institute for International Economics, 1989).

16. The classic locus of this critique is Joseph Stiglitz, *Globalization and Its Discontents* (New York: W.W. Norton & Co, 2002).

17. Dani Rodrik, "Goodbye Washington Consensus, Hello Washington Confusion?" in *Journal of Economic Literature* 44 (2006).

18. For example, Alexander Gerschenkron, *Economic Backwardness in Historical Perspective* (Cambridge, MA: Harvard University Press, 1962).

19. Peter Navarro, *The Coming China Wars: Where They Will Be Fought and How They Can Be Won* (Upper Saddle River, NJ: FT Press, 2006); *Death by China: Confronting the Dragon—A Global Call to Action* (Upper Saddle River, NJ: FT Press, 2011).

CHAPTER 2

ON THE FUTURE OF CAPITALISM IN EUROPE

KAI A. KONRAD[1]

CRITIQUE OF CAPITALISM

Does the capitalist system have a future? If you search for "future of capitalism" on Google, you will find lots of answers to this question. For example, in a 2016 interview with *Die Zeit*, the philosopher Patrick Spät said that capitalism is based on exploitation and is destroying itself.[2] In expressing this theory, Spät joins a long tradition. The fundamental theme of "exploitation" has been repeated many times in the history of the critique of capitalism and has been a key topos since Karl Marx. By contrast, more specific reasons for the self-destruction of the capitalist system have varied over the past 200 years or so. Equally, the social scientist Wolfgang Streeck[3] considers that the question of whether capitalism is coming to an end has already been answered. He directly addresses the question of how capitalism will end, and in doing so identifies five problem areas: "The capitalist system suffers from at least five deteriorating dysfunctions, against which there is currently no effective remedy: a deceleration in growth, oligarchy, starvation of the public sphere, corruption, and anarchy on an international scale."

CAPITALISM—A SUCCESS STORY?

In light of the facts, the vehemence of the opposition to and the large number of general criticisms of the capitalist economic system should be surprising. After all, this economic system successfully prevailed over an economic and social system that was based on personal relationships extending even as far as serfdom: capitalism replaced the feudal system—a system that for its unequal distribution of power, income, and assets is hard to beat.[4] The system of market economy can attest to enormous successes. The psychologist and public intellectual Steven Pinker provides an astonishing abundance of illustrations.[5] According to Pinker, living conditions on Earth have improved significantly over the past 200 years in many respects; indeed for many parts of the world and for very broad strata of the population. He refers to studies showing that the proportion of the global population who live in "extreme poverty" fell from 90 percent to 10 percent between 1820 and today. Half of this decline, he says, took place in the last 35 years alone. In addition, he cites studies that show a massive decrease in inequality throughout the world and a dramatic increase in social spending as a share of gross domestic product in OECD countries. Other indicators also suggest that many economic and technological developments of the last two hundred years have been beneficial not to a small elite but to broad strata of the population. He mentions, among other things, improvements in protection against accidents and life-threatening risks and the reduction in violent crime and armed conflict, and not least the huge increase in life expectancy.

All these developments do not quite fit the picture of a system that is struggling with collapse and based on a system of exploitation. And here we should point out that Pinker's book addresses the benefits of the Enlightenment, not those of capitalism. It is, however, difficult to attribute causality. In fact, the developments he summarizes take place in the era of a market-based economic system with private property, i.e. the era of capitalism. In any case, the reward mechanisms in such a system and the scope for economic development that this economic system offers can be considered as possible triggers for and agents of these positive developments.

Anyone educated in modern economics who reads the prophecies of capitalism's decline will come across one fact in particular. Many of the reasons given have absolutely no place in a description of the constituent elements of the capitalist economic system. A capitalist economic system is based on three fundamental principles. First, the idea of individualism. The key actors and decision-makers in the system are those who appreciate their "self," not families, clans, or other collectives, for example. Second, the principle of private property. Individuals have property rights, that is the power to control their goods. Private property covers consumer goods, but also tools, machines, one's own labor, talent, one's own body and mind. Third, there is contractual freedom. Individuals have freedom of disposition over their property; they can consume it, produce with it, give it away or sell it;

they can also enter into contracts with other individuals by which they regulate the transfer and exchange of property. And they bear the consequences of their actions as individuals.

However, such an economic system needs a guaranteeing authority. The latter must ensure that private property, individual rights of disposal and decision-making and the individual's contractual freedom are not undermined by other individuals. Arbitrary political decisions must also be prevented. The functioning of a private-sector system of market economy stands or falls with the existence of appropriate legal and political frameworks. It is here, and thus beyond the actual market economy, private-sector sphere, where the real problems facing the functioning of a capitalist system probably lie.[6]

THE CURRENT CHALLENGES

In the years and decades to come, as many experts tell us, rapid technological advances in many areas (artificial intelligence, robotics, biotechnology) will lead to major changes. These changes harbor great opportunities, but they also entail major upheavals. A private-sector system of market economy may perhaps provide the best institutional response to these challenges. In any case, it has great potential for adapting swiftly to changed circumstances. However, it is questionable whether the political and social system that currently exists in Western industrialized countries is prepared to guarantee the legal and political framework for the continued existence of this system of market economy.

The continent of Europe can respond to these challenges through two fundamentally different strategies: "adaptation" and "defense." The adaptation strategy reacts with openness to the changing possibilities. It creates frameworks that enable the individual to seize the opportunities offered by technological progress. It supports initiative, encourages training and transformation in the labor market, makes it easier for pioneering entrepreneurs to enter the market, and simplifies the innovation of new products and markets. It thus enables the creation of new jobs and employment opportunities for broad sections of the population.

The dynamics of adaptation, however, have considerable explosive social consequences, because many established professions and whole economic sectors might become obsolete. Expert systems based on artificial intelligence are competing with workers in many traditional occupations—translators, truck drivers, and taxi drivers, for example. Such systems also replace labor-intensive processes in medical diagnostics, tax consultancy, and possibly many other industries. To allay the resulting explosive social consequences, new products, new industries, and new, productive occupations must be created on a large scale. This can only happen within a society that is open to adaptation and change.

As China has exemplified over the past decades, it is possible to undertake such adaptations with great rapidity. In just a few decades, China's economy, country, and population have transformed from an agricultural economy into a modern industrial society. In doing do, China has lived through three industrial revolutions at high speed. In just a few decades, the country developed from one of the poorest economies into a major economic powerhouse. An important phase in this process was when China, as a low-wage country, produced consumer goods for the developed world. Western industrial companies paid for them with machinery and high-tech goods. There are many indications that this economic era is coming to an end. Today, China aspires to play a leading role in some technological sectors. The country is pursuing a long-term economic policy with its strategic investments in neighboring countries, in the continent of Africa, and even in Western industrialized societies. It is remarkable that these economic revolutions successfully brought about a market economy whose guarantor is a political system that is autocratic in character.

There are signs that many developed economies, especially in Europe, are struggling with dynamic adjustment. Many industries in Europe are in defensive mode. The theories developed by Mancur Olson offer systematic reasons for this.[7] He points out that as the political system gets older, an ever denser network of increasingly organized groups emerges. Each of these groups is pursuing its own distributional interests. They exert an influence on the political process with the aim of maintaining or securing a larger share of the total national income. These groups include industry and trade associations, professional associations, trade unions, and many others. Over time, these powerful and well-organized associations gain massive influence over politics and society. However, economic and technological development, as Joseph Schumpeter put it, is a process of creative destruction. Specific sectors of the old economy are thus the losers in this change, even if overall this transformation may bring major gains in prosperity. Accordingly, individual interest groups focus their power and influence on preventing this change. They protect their interests very effectively, but in so doing drastically reduce the adaptability of the entire system. As Olson describes, the accumulation of groups with specific distributional interests is leading to an increasingly complex political system and a proliferation of interlinked regulatory requirements. This has negative consequences for social and societal development and for the question of how business, society, and politics react to technological progress and other challenges. Vito Tanzi, the long-time Director of the Fiscal Affairs Department at the International Monetary Fund, has also come to similar conclusions. In his book *Termites of the State*,[8] he compares the erosion of states' political structures with the infestation of buildings by termites, which becomes apparent when it is basically too late to enact countermeasures.

PERSPECTIVES

On a trip to China in fall 2017, I was greeted at Beijing Airport by a wall-sized photo of Venice. In romantic evening light, it showed the view from the Rialto Bridge across the Grand Canal—probably a favorite destination for many Chinese people. In his account of the history of Venice,[9] Frederic C. Lane describes a city that, over the course of long periods of geopolitical change and the development of new technologies in the maritime trade, helped shape these changes. For centuries, the city enjoyed prosperity and was one of the economic and political centers of the world. Venice's former greatness has long since been a thing of the past. Although it is still reflected in the buildings, the Venice of today is primarily a tourist destination.

Today, the continent of Europe too is threatened by such a development, at the very moment when its various interest groups are successfully fighting against transformations in the political sphere instead of embracing the transformation and making the most of the new opportunities, and also when such transformations are being rejected by society at large. Like Venice, old Europe might become a tourist destination in the decades to come, with millions of Chinese travelers visiting the buildings and artefacts that bear witness to Europe's faded economic and political greatness, and the glitter of its past centuries of success.

Notes

1. This essay is an extended version of my opinion piece that was published in 2018 under the title "Die Zukunft des Kapitalismus" in issue 32 of *Focus magazine.*

2. Zeit-Online, https://www.zeit.de/karriere/2016-07/ka-pitalismus-industrie-4-0-digitalisierung-zukunft-arbeits-markt-kritik/seite-2 (accessed December 4, 2018).

3. Cf. Wolfgang Streek, "Wie wird der Kapitalismus enden?" Part II in *Blätter für deutsche und internationale Politik* 4 (2015), p. 120.

4. For its part, this previous system had prevailed against a world of competing, small mutual benefit societies. On this previous system and its establishment, see Marc Bloch, *Feudal Society*, trans. L.A. Manyon (Oxford: Routledge, 2014).

5. Steven Pinker, *Enlightenment Now: The Case for Reason, Science, Humanism, and Progress* (New York: Allen Lane, 2018).

6. In this context, we refer to the pioneering work on an economy without such guarantees by Trygve Haavelmo, *A Study in the Theory of Economic Evolution* (New York: North Holland Publishing, 1964).

7. Cf. Mancur Olson, *The Rise and Decline of Nations: Economic Growth, Stagflation, and Social Rigidities* (New Haven, CT: Yale University Press, 1982).

8. Cf. Vito Tanzi, *Termites of the State* (New York: Cambridge University Press, 2018).

9. Cf. Frederic C. Lane, *Venice: A Maritime Republic* (Baltimore, MD: The Johns Hopkins University Press, 1973).

CHAPTER 3

ON THE IMPORTANCE OF GROSS DOMESTIC PRODUCT AND GROWTH

JÖRG ROCHOLL

For many years, the usefulness of economic growth has been the subject of intense economic and political debate, during which many arguments have been put forward in favor of sustained economic growth. Politicians in Germany often refer, not without pride, to the lasting economic boom. Even in 2017, gross domestic product (GDP) continued to increase.[1] At the same time, a series of questions arises, such as whether the increasing prosperity of the global population leads to the excessive consumption of natural resources. In response, the first critics of growth could be heard as early as the 1970s. In their view, a deliberate slowdown in economic growth is the only way out of the prosperity dilemma. Degrowth, post-growth, growth reduction—there are many names but no generally accepted definition of the process operating to counter the kind of growth that overstretches resources. The *Frankfurter Allgemeine Zeitung* describes degrowth or post-growth as "progressive alternatives to the diktat of growth."[2] Proponents characterize degrowth as "the reduction in consumption and production, and thus also gross domestic product, as a way of achieving more social justice, environmental sustainability, and welfare."[3]

This essay deals with two important aspects of this debate: First, we aim to establish whether gross domestic product is a suitable measure of prosperity; then we discuss whether the growth of prosperity is desirable.

1. GROSS DOMESTIC PRODUCT AS A MEASURE OF PROSPERITY

For some time, it has been acknowledged that GDP is limited as a measure of a society's prosperity. As early as 1968, Robert Kennedy said:

We seemed to have surrendered personal excellence and community values in the mere accumulation of material things. Our Gross National Product, now, is over $800 billion dollars a year, but that Gross National Product [...] counts air pollution and cigarette advertising, and ambulances to clear our highways of carnage. [...] Yet the gross national product does not allow for the health of our children, the quality of their education or the joy of their play [...] it measures everything in short, except that which makes life worthwhile.[4]

In a similar vein, the financial magazine *The Economist* argued in 2016: "[The] gross domestic product (GDP) is increasingly a poor measure of prosperity. It is not a reliable gauge of production."[5] The article lists a number of limitations, including the lack of measurement of the quality of goods and services consumed and the innovations they contain, as well as the lack of recognition of voluntary work. The failure to account for services that are not traded on markets or that are provided free of charge as they are unpriced, as well as the inadequate recognition of sustainability issues, i.e., the failure to discount essential, existential variables such as the environment or health, leads, in the calculation of GDP, to either the underestimation or the overestimation of actual prosperity.

Thus, since gross domestic product alone does not allow for overarching, reliable statements about a country's prosperity, a number of other factors must be enlisted which together make it possible to compare the prosperity of various countries. In 2008, the then French President Nicolas Sarkozy convened the Stiglitz-Sen-Fitoussi Commission, named for its chairmen, to discuss the problem of GDP as a unit of measurement. The commission divided the topic into three areas—economic indicators, quality of life, and sustainability/environment—and made a total of twelve core recommendations. In addition to measuring well-being through level of income and consumption, and recognizing the correlation between income and consumption, factors such as capabilities and distribution of wealth also have an influence here. The commission came to the conclusion that taking GDP alone as a measure of prosperity is too narrow.

Nevertheless, there are good reasons to argue that, despite all its limitations, GDP should still be taken on board as an important indicator. GDP remains relevant as a value in itself because it is closely related to obligations such as paying down national debt. Paying down such debt becomes all the easier as GDP increases. The same applies to coping with the burdens of both implicit debt (for example, in pay-as-you-go pension and social security schemes) and adaptation costs incurred by climate change. Last but not least, GDP correlates closely with other welfare indicators, such as the Human Development Index (HDI) developed by the United Nations, which includes not only income but also education and health indicators. Also, the high correlation of GDP with life expectancy suggests that rising incomes are a precondition of progress in other areas as well.[6] Even the findings that rising incomes did not lead to greater happiness (known as the Easterlin Paradox) have now been challenged or revised by widely acclaimed recent work.[7] In any case, the debate on this issue goes on.[8]

2. THREE REASONS FOR GROWTH

As a concept, growth *per se* has positive connotations. But how do you determine the need and the reasons for growth? The first reason arguing in favor of economic growth is based on the obvious goal of reducing global poverty. In 2013, the German Economic Institute (IW) published a short report on the fight against poverty:

> People who have to live with a purchasing power of less than 1.25 USD per day are considered to be in extreme poverty. In 1990, according to this

definition, 43 percent of the global population lived in extreme poverty. In 2010, this proportion is only 21 percent—while in the same period the global population increased by 1.8 billion. The number of people in poverty has therefore fallen from more than 1.9 billion to around 1.2 billion.[9]

The United Nations has thus achieved its goal of halving poverty between 1990 and 2015. In response, that same year the World Bank formulated a new goal: by 2030, it intends to ensure that a maximum of 3 percent of the global population has to manage on less than 1.90 USD per day.[10] To do this, we must recognize and promote the reasons why the earlier economic consolidation succeeded. According to IW, these reasons are, above all, economic growth and justice. According to estimates, economic growth of 1 percent per year can reduce poverty by an average of 1.7 percent. International trade and globalization of the market are helping to lower poverty rates over the long term. In China, for example, the poverty rate decreased from 84 percent in 1980 to 10 percent in 2013. Fairer wealth distribution within a country can further encourage the reduction of poverty rates. *The Economist* argues that poverty in countries with more equal distribution decreases more strongly with every 1 percent of economic growth than in those where wealth is unevenly distributed. Nevertheless, an equal distribution of wealth alone is not enough: "Reliable institutions and an infrastructure that benefits everyone are also aids to reducing poverty."[11]

A second important reason for the need for economic growth is the potential impact of natural disasters. Developing countries in particular need growth in order to protect against the consequences of climate change and the attendant growing probability of natural disasters. Nobel laureate Thomas Schelling argues as follows:

> Developing Nations have the most to lose from climate change. [...]. Constrained by poverty and economical backwardness, their ability to adapt to climate change is limited. The best way for developing countries to adapt to climate change, therefore, is through economic growth. [...] If there was aid to divide between Singapore and Bangladesh, would anybody propose giving any of it to Singapore? In 50 to 75 years, when climate change may be a realistic reality, Bangladesh probably will have progressed to the level of Singapore today.[12] Should anyone propose investing heavily in the welfare of those future Bangladeshis when the alternative is to help Bangladesh today?[13]

Countries such as Bangladesh, which as a result of climate change are facing increasingly frequent and more severe natural disasters, need better financial resources to absorb these catastrophes. For these countries, economic growth is desirable and almost indispensable in order to be better prepared in the long term.

A third important reason for economic growth arises from the question of how best to deal with national debt that has accumulated over many decades. There are basically six possible solutions for reducing national debt, for example: "The first solution for getting rid of debt through economic growth is the most desirable, but at the same time the most difficult to realize."[14] Austerity and the transfer of debt to other countries encounter so much resistance that they cannot be realistically implemented. For creditors, debt restructuring is associated with losses, and therefore just as difficult to implement. And a substantial rate of inflation, which can reduce debt in real terms while also reducing wealth in real terms, will inevitably meet with resistance. The last solution is thus financial repression. According to Reinhart, Kirkegaard, and Sbrancia, this can be summarized in the following three options:

1. "Explicit or indirect caps or ceilings on interest rates, particularly [...] those on government debts

2. Creation and maintenance of a captive domestic audience

3. Other common measures [...] are, direct ownership (China or India) of banks or extensive management of banks and other financial institutions (i.e. Japan). Restrictions of entry to the financial industry and directing credit to certain industries are also features [...]."[15]

This last option is also associated with even more unpleasant consequences than economic growth.

3. ON THE CONSUMPTION OF RESOURCES

Critics have traditionally pointed to the negative impact of economic growth on the consumption of resources. This critique is based on the fundamental idea that a global population that is becoming ever more prosperous can and wants to afford more and more material things. However, this is countered by the economic principle that a growing demand for resources increases the scarcity of these resources, which increases their market price. In turn, the rising market price increases the incentive to look for alternatives. Often such alternatives have not only been found quickly, but have even turned out to be markedly superior. One of the countless examples is replacing copper cables with fiber-optic cables.

Thus, more prosperity does not necessarily mean a greater consumption of resources. Indeed, the opposite is frequently true, because innovation and increasing efficiency can actually decrease the consumption of resources despite increasing prosperity. For example, absolute oil consumption in Germany has fallen by more than 20 percent over the last 20 years, while gross domestic product has risen by about 25 percent in the same period.[16] In fact, in many areas today, qualitative rather than quantitative growth is already taking place.

In addition, many resource problems that seem very important at the time could be almost completely solved through technology and innovative inventions. In London in 1894, for example, the Great Horse Manure Crisis led to a *Times* article predicting: "In 50 years, every street in London will be under nine feet of manure."[17] By 1915, the last horse-drawn tram in London had been replaced by an electric version.[18]

Moreover, innovative technologies ("green tech") and the correct internalization of external effects (for example, in the case of climate protection) make so-called "green growth" imaginable. Awareness of the sustainability of resources should be created everywhere, but in countries with very high growth rates especially, the responsible use of resources should be promoted at an early stage.

4. IS THERE AN INHERENT GROWTH DIKTAT IN MARKET ECONOMIES?

Does this mean that economic growth is unstoppable? In a market economy, goods and services, for which there is a demand, are produced. If the demand for goods declines overall (for example, because of the emergence of greater preferences for leisure time), a natural decline in growth is in principle possible (for example, in the metals industry, collectively agreed working hours have fallen by more than a third in the last 60 years).[19] Nevertheless, growth is not a decision variable, but rather a target variable. It is produced by creativity, mutually beneficial trade, and work—that is through human endeavors. Arbitrary interventions, for example imposing a reduction in weekly working hours to 20 hours,[20] as demanded by radical growth critics, represent a huge infringement of freedom and could quickly lead to an authoritarian system.

5. SUMMARY

The debate about economic growth versus degrowth continues today, and this essay illustrates several important aspects of it. On the one hand, we argue that gross domestic product, as a measure of prosperity, does indeed have its limitations, but nevertheless remains meaningful. Particularly in conjunction with other measured data such as the HDI and taking into account other parameters, gross domestic product remains a reliable factor, because it resists manipulation and is thus not subject to the arbitrariness the individual.

On the other hand, this essay describes the importance of economic growth in coping with the consequences of climate change by improving the financial resources of poorer countries in particular. For countries that are less developed than the EU states, continued economic growth and a consistent increase in prosperity are also the essential precondition for paving their population's way out of poverty. Finally, an increase in prosperity is desirable for those countries that are heavily indebted. An increase in gross domestic product greatly facilitates the repayment of their national debt.

Notes

1. https://www.destatis.de/DE/PresseService/Presse/ Pressemitteilungen/2018/01/PD18_011_811.html (accessed October 9, 2018).

2. http://www.faz.net/aktuell/wirtschaft/ wirtschaftswissen/postwachstumsgesellschaft-und-degrowth-neue-konzepte-der-oekonomie-14493710.html (accessed October 11, 2018).

3. https://www.nachhaltigkeit.info/artikel/degrowth_1849. htm (accessed October 11, 2018).

4. https://www.theguardian.com/news/datablog/2012/ may/24/robert-kennedy-gdp (accessed October 4, 2018).

5. https://www.economist.com/briefing/2016/04/30/the-trouble-with-gdp (accessed October 5, 2018).

6. https://www.gapminder.org/news/hdi-surprisingly-similar-to-gdpcapita/ (accessed October 5, 2018).

7. Betsey Stevenson and Justin Wolfers, "Economic Growth and Subjective Well-Being: Reassessing the Easterlin Paradox" in *Brookings Papers on Economic Activity, Economic Studies Program, The Brookings Institution*, vol. 39 (1), 2008, pp. 1–102. http://www.nber.org/papers/w14282 (accessed October 8, 2018).

8. https://www.brookings.edu/opinions/debunking-the-easterlin-paradox-again/ (accessed October 11, 2018).

9. Institut der deutschen Wirtschaft, IW-Kurzbericht, *Wachstum hilft den Schwachen*, 2013. https://www.iwkoeln. de/studien/iw-kurzberichte/beitrag/armutsbekaempfung-wachstum-hilft-den-schwachen-118242.html (accessed October 11, 2018).

10. http://www.worldbank.org/en/news/feature/2013/04/17/ ending_extreme_poverty_and_promoting_shared_ prosperity (accessed October 10, 2018).

11. https://www.iwkoeln.de/studien/iw-kurzberichte/ beitrag/armutsbekaempfung-wachstum-hilft-den-schwachen-118242.html (accessed October 10, 2018).

12. This article was published in 1997.

13. https://worldisgreen.wordpress.com/2007/07/12/thomas-schelling-on-climate-change/amp/ (accessed October 11, 2018).

14. Jörg Rocholl, "Unternehmensfinanzierung im Licht des finanzwirtschaftlichen Strukturwandels" in Michael Hüther, Knut Bergmann, and Dominik H. Enste (eds.), *Unternehmen im öffentlichen Raum: Zwischen Markt und Mitverantwortung* (Heidelberg: Springer, 2014/15), pp. 185–98.

15. Ibid., p. 193.

16. https://www.statista.com/statistics/262843/development-of-oil-consumption-in-germany/ (accessed October 10, 2018); https://de.statista.com/statistik/daten/studie/ 1251/umfrage/entwicklung-des-bruttoinlandsprodukts-seit-dem-jahr-1991/ (accessed October 11, 2018).

17. Cf. https://www.ft.com/content/238b1038-13bb-11e3-9289-00144feabdc0 (accessed October 9, 2018).

18. https://en.wikipedia.org/wiki/Trams_in_London (accessed October 9, 2018).

19. https://metall.nrw/fileadmin/std_project/content_data/ Downloads/Kommunikation/iwd/IWD_2016-25_ Seite_10-11.pdf (accessed October 11, 2018).

20. https://www.zeit.de/wirtschaft/2017-01/europa-fortschritt-wachstum-industrie-digitalisierung-oekologie-klimawandel (accessed October 11, 2018).

CHAPTER 4

THE POLITICS OF GROWTH MODELS

LUCIO BACCARO

Based on joint work with Jonas Pontusson (Baccaro and Pontusson 2016, Baccaro and Pontusson 2018a; Baccaro and Pontusson 2018b), this essay explores different ways in which advanced countries generate growth. Growth is a very important political goal for governments, since it facilitates reelection and assuages distributive conflict. The main point of the essay is to argue that there is no single growth model, but there are different ones. Let us begin with an examination of cross-country trends.

INTERNATIONAL TRENDS

As argued elsewhere (Baccaro and Howell 2017; Baccaro and Howell 2018), advanced capitalist economies are characterized by three common tendencies: 1. A generalized trend of liberalization of economic institutions, especially labor market institutions (unionization, centralized collective bargaining, employment protection, etc.); 2. A generalized shift in the distribution of functional income away from labor income and towards capital income broadly defined. There is a declining trend of the labor share of GDP in all G7 countries, although the starting point of the decline varies (between the mid-1970s and mid-1980s) and there is some sign, for example in Italy, that the decline may have plateaued; 3. An increasing difficulty of all advanced countries to generate adequate levels of aggregate demand to employ factors of production, notably labor. This phenomenon goes under the name of "secular stagnation" and was recently brought to international attention by Larry Summers (Summers 2014).

It may be hypothesized that the three trends do not just overlap temporally, but stand in a causal relationship to one another. The liberalization of labor institutions is at least partly responsible for the distributional shift. There is some evidence of this particular link in econometric research (Kristal 2010). Furthermore, the decline of the wage share tends to generate a "leak" in aggregate demand, in the sense that the demand for consumer goods and services in the economy tends to stagnate, while the demand for financial assets, and the associated search for yield, increases. These trends have an important impact on growth models, since they affect the viability of the "wage-led" model of growth.

WAGE-LED GROWTH AND ITS DECLINE

Until approximately 1990, i.e. in the pre-globalization phase, all large European countries grew based on a variant of the wage-led growth model (Lavoie and Stockhammer 2013). In a wage-led growth model, real wages grow at the same rate (or even slightly faster) than labor productivity increases, thus feeding household consumption. The prospect of an expanding demand, in turn, stimulates firms to invest. This tends to increase productivity, since the new investments incorporate the latest generation of technical progress. Furthermore, expanding demand enables economies of scale, which is another mechanism (already known to Adam Smith) by which labor productivity increases.

The wage-led growth model no longer exists in its original, institutionalized form. It has been undermined by both domestic and international developments. First, wage pressures had a tendency to produce inflation, which was difficult to contain through attempts at wage and price controls. Eventually, the fight against inflation led to a series of policy and institutional reforms, including the introduction of inflation-targeting central banks, which made it difficult for real wages to grow at the same rate as productivity (Glyn 2006). Second, the liberalization of capital movements made it impossible for national policy-making authorities to reduce interest rates (adjusted for inflation) below the level prevailing in international markets. This made investments more sensitive to profit rates. Finally, the expansion of international trade increased the systemic importance of wage moderation. *Real* wage moderation tends to slow down the economy in a wage-led growth model, but *nominal* wage moderation, if it leads to lower domestic inflation than in trade partners and if it is not counterbalanced by nominal exchange rate appreciation, stimulates net exports. For sufficiently open economies, wage moderation becomes expansionary, i.e. the depressive effect on domestic demand is more than compensated by the expansionary effect on net exports.

It should be emphasized that the wage-led growth model was implemented differently in various different countries. One major dimension of national diversity was the presence of institutions for centralized wage negotiations, in which large and encompassing trade unions and employer associations would more easily internalize the importance of spontaneous wage moderation and thus reduce the inflation rate with a lesser need for costly disinflation through restrictive monetary policy (Tarantelli 1986).

THE EMERGENCE OF NEW GROWTH MODELS IN THE PRE-CRISIS PERIOD

The theoretical framework Jonas Pontusson and I have developed, the Growth Models (GM) perspective, seeks to account for both common trends and national peculiarities in advanced capitalisms (Baccaro and Pontusson 2016; 2018b). In so doing, unlike most theories in comparative political economy, it underplays the role of institutional differences across countries (for example, in the structure of the collective bargaining system, or of the welfare state, or of corporate governance), and focuses instead on different "demand drivers." This implies a return to Keynes, an author whose importance for comparative political economy had declined in the past few decades, and a return of aggregate demand to the spotlight.

Another key element of the GM perspective is the incorporation of Kalecki's view that aggregate demand depends on the distribution of labor and capital income. This is due to different propensities to consume and, conversely, to save between receivers of labor income (who tend to consume a greater proportion of it) and receivers of capital income (who tend to save it in greater proportion). In the Keynesian–Kaleckian framework, a distributional shift in favor of capital means lower demand for goods and services and higher demand for financial assets. An increase in savings, in turn, does not necessarily stimulate investment by reducing the interest rate. Rather, the equality between savings and investment is brought about by GDP adjustment (shrinking).

A further element of the GM perspective is borrowed from Kalecki. It consists in the claim that although functional distribution also depends on other factors, it is shaped by politics, and specifically by the balance of power between labor and capital in the labor market. In fact, the wage share of output is equivalent to the real wage divided by labor productivity, and thus developments in the wage share may be interpreted as resulting from the ability of real wages to keep up with productivity increases, which in turn is a function of the bargaining power of workers.

In an economy in which growth is wage-led, and all large European economies are wage-led according to recent econometric estimates (Onaran and Galanis 2014), a declining wage share generates a problem of insufficient aggregate demand. This leads policy-making elites at national level to look for alternative demand drivers of growth. Two alternatives can be observed: in the first alternative, the economy continues to be pulled by household consumption as in the old wage-led model, but consumption is financed not so much by real wages, but rather by easier access to debt by households. In the second alternative, the growth driver becomes net foreign demand and the associated trade surpluses. However, it is perfectly possible that no alternative growth driver is found, and in this case the outcome is protracted stagnation.

Focusing on Germany, Italy, Sweden, and the UK in the 15 years before the Global Financial Crisis, four different growth models emerge: a consumption-led model epitomized by the UK, an export-led model epitomized by Germany, an export- plus consumption-led model in Sweden, and the neither export- nor consumption-led model of Italy (Baccaro and Pontusson 2016).

If one looks at the yearly contribution of net exports to growth in five-year averages between 1994 and 2007, one sees that this contribution was increasing in Germany, positive and stable, albeit somewhat declining in the later period in Sweden, negligible overall in Italy, and negative in the UK. If then one considers the contribution of household consumption to growth, one sees that this was highly positive in the UK, positive in Sweden, declining in Italy, declining and negligible in the latest period in Germany. Thus, the growth drivers were net exports in Germany, household consumption in the UK, both drivers were present in Sweden and neither one was present in Italy, which effectively stagnated (the data and graphs illustrating the above statements can be found in Baccaro and Pontusson [2016]).

Let us now examine the most important features of each growth model. Easier access to credit enabled "consumption-led" growth in the UK in the pre-crisis period. Interestingly, buoyant household consumption tends to create favorable labor market conditions, including for low- and semi-skilled service workers, such that real wage growth is greater than in alternative growth models. However, unlike a wage-led growth model, there is no autonomous wage push, but wage growth is derivative from market conditions.

A distinctive feature of the consumption-led growth model is the tendency to accumulate current account deficits. In normal circumstances, these deficits would need to be corrected by reducing internal demand and imports. However, if the rest of the world is willing to finance the current account deficit, it may be sustainable over many years. A large and liquid financial hub such as the City of London, which produces financial assets that the rest of the world wants to hold in its portfolio, contributes to attracting foreign capital and thus to relaxing the current account constraint for growth.

Germany's "export-led" growth model is almost the opposite of the consumption-led model. It is based on three elements: an export sector large enough to act as locomotive for the economy as a whole, institutionalized wage moderation, and a fixed exchange rate regime. The latter two elements lead to real exchange rate underappreciation (Hoepner 2018), which tends to stimulate exports and depress imports. The German growth model has not always been an export-led one, but shifted to export-led sometime in the 15 years preceding the Great Recession (Baccaro and Benassi 2017). During these years, while the contribution of net exports to German growth was mounting, the contribution of household consumption was declining. There was a seeming trade-off between the former and the latter: wage moderation and the decline of the wage share contributed to boost net exports via the reduction of demand and the effect on the real exchange rate. The burden of adjustment was unequally distributed for German workers: while the real wages of manufacturing workers remained more or less indexed to economy-wide productivity, the real wages of low-skilled service workers did not increase.

Sweden's growth model was able to combine the consumption driver and the export driver of growth until before the crisis, while it became more consumption-oriented after the crisis. There is some evidence that Swedish exports are less price sensitive than German exports and, as such, there is no need for the type of wage and consumption repression experienced in Germany (Baccaro and Pontusson 2016). Unlike the German economy, in which manufacturing main-tained a predominant position, Swedish exports became more differentiated, with the IT and high-value-added service sectors becoming more impor-tant. These sectors are presumably less price sensitive than manufacturing. Simultaneously, growing house-hold indebtedness also stimulated consumption. Real wage growth was not just higher than in Germany, but also more equally distributed between high-end manufacturing and low-end services.

The Italian case illustrates that it is possible for a country to be unable to find a viable replacement for wage-led growth and thus to stagnate. The contribution of household consumption to growth declined over time in Italy. The contribution of exports has recently increased, but the Italian export sector is still too small to be a significant growth driver, and net exports are weighed down by a real exchange rate that is too high for the country's needs (due to the Euro).

For exports to play the role of growth driver, they have to account for a large percentage of GDP. German exports grew much faster as a percentage of GDP than Italian and British exports from the mid-1990s on, eventually catching up with Sweden (which is a much smaller country). Household debt, another possible driver of growth, was approximately the same as the percentage of net disposable income in the mid-1990s in Britain, Germany, and Sweden. Italy's households were instead less indebted than others. In the pre-crisis period, British and Swedish debt continued to increase (Swedish household debt increased even after the crisis), while German debt declined. Italian debt also increased but probably not sufficiently to rekindle consumption significantly.

Real wages grew much more in Britain (in the pre-crisis period) and Sweden than in Germany and

Italy. There seems to have been a drastic change in the German wage-setting system. If one distinguishes between high-end manufacturing (which excluded the textile and apparel sector) and low-end services (retail; hotels and restaurants), one sees that between 1974 and 1990, real wages in high-end manufacturing and low-end services grew more or less in line with each other, and in line with the increase of labor productivity. This is what one would expect from a coordinated bargaining system. Between 1991 and 2007, however, manufacturing real wages grew more or less in line with labor productivity, at least until the mid-2000s, but real wages in low-end services were flat and even slightly declining (see Baccaro and Pontusson 2016). Clearly, wage moderation was unequally distributed across German sectors.

SOCIAL BLOCS AND PARTY POLITICS

The last part of this essay deals with the politics of growth models. What type of social coalitions under-pins different demand drivers of growth? The key idea here is that growth models are based on "dominant social blocs." These are coalitions of large firms and skilled workers in "key" sectors, i.e. sectors that have a systemic importance for their contribution to aggregate demand or to the country's capacities for innovation and productivity improvement (for example, the export-oriented manufacturing sector in Germany). One characteristic of dominant social blocs is that they produce a legitimating discourse, i.e. they are able to present the interests of the bloc as coinciding with the national interest.

Key sectors have distinct "requirements" and these requirements, to the extent that the sector is part of the dominant social bloc, will be incorporated in and accommodated by public policy, especially macroeconomic policy. One well-known distinction is between sectors exposed to international competition and sectors protected from international competition. These two sectors face two very different sources of demand: foreign demand in the former case; domestic demand in the latter. The factors that stimulate these two types of demand are also different: relative prices and technological excellence in the former case; income distribution and social policies in the latter. A less appreciated sectoral distinction is between real interest rate-sensitive sectors such as construction, and real exchange rate-sensitive sectors such as (some areas of) manufacturing. For the former, all other things being equal, higher inflation leads to lower real interest rates which stimulate demand for the sectoral output. For the latter, higher inflation (if the nominal exchange rate is prevented from adjusting due to fixed exchange rates or a single currency) is detrimental because it makes imports cheaper and exports more expensive. Thus sectoral actors should have different preferences about the monetary, fiscal, exchange rate, and wage policies which impact on inflation.

A particularly interesting case is the possibility of a coincidence of interests between the construction sector and the parts of the financial sector specializing in mortgage finance. As argued above, the construction sector should not be too concerned about inflation, but research shows that the finance sector is deeply inflation-averse, since inflation tends to erode the real value of highly liquid assets (Mosley 2003). However, the two interests can be reconciled if housing prices and general prices are decoupled, i.e. if the former grow rapidly while the latter grow moderately, and this is likely to happen if nominal wage growth is kept low due to weak unions, weak labor protections, and precarious employment.

Party politics plays an important role in the politics of growth models, because in most circumstances the dominant social bloc fails to control 50 percent of the votes directly, and needs to construct an electoral majority around the policies that benefit the social bloc. The assumption of the GM perspective is that mainstream parties compete in terms of their ability to manage the growth model and associated social bloc, not in terms of fundamentally different alternatives (at least when the growth model is clearly defined). In other words, there is an expectation that mainstream parties will converge around policies that are beneficial for the social bloc. This hypothesis resonates with the "party cartelization" thesis in political science (Katz and Mair 1995). Parties contribute to stabilizing the social bloc in two ways: by striking interest-based alliances with social groups outside the core, to which some of the proceedings of growth are redistributed, and also, importantly, through the cultural reinterpretation of individual and group preferences. The hypothesis here, to be tested in future research, is that groups in similar socioeconomic conditions (for example construction workers in an export-led and a consumption-led economy) will express different preferences about the desirability of policy (about the importance of wage moderation) depending on the persuasive power of different definitions of the "national interest."

References

Baccaro, Lucio and Jonas Pontusson. 2016. "Rethinking Comparative Political Economy: The Growth Model Perspective." *Politics & Society* 44 (2): 175–207. doi: 10.1177/0032329216638053.

Baccaro, Lucio and Chiara Benassi. 2017. "Throwing out the Ballast: Growth Models and the Liberalization of German Industrial Relations." *Socio-Economic Review* 15 (1): 85–115. doi:10.1093/ser/mww036.

Baccaro, Lucio and Chris Howell. 2017. *Trajectories of Neoliberal Transformation: European Industrial Relations after the 1970s.* Cambridge, UK: Cambridge University Press.

Baccaro, Lucio and Chris Howell. 2018. "Unhinged: Industrial Relations Liberalization and Capitalist Instability." MPIfG Discussion Paper 17/19.

Baccaro, Lucio and Jonas Pontusson. 2018a. "Comparative Capitalisms and Macroeconomics." Unpublished paper, University of Geneva.

Baccaro, Lucio and Jonas Pontusson. 2018b. "The Politics of Growth in Germany and Sweden." Paper presented at Workshop on "Pushing the Growth Models Agenda Forward," Max Planck Institute, Cologne, May 24–25.

Glyn, Andrew. 2006. *Capitalism Unleashed : Finance Globalization and Welfare.* Oxford/New York: Oxford University Press.

Hoepner, Martin. 2018. "The German Undervaluation Regime under Bretton Woods, 1950–1973: How Germany Became the Nightmare of the World Economy." Unpublished paper, Max-Planck Institut für Gesellschaftsforschung.

Katz, Richard S. and Peter Mair. 1995. "The Changing Models of Party Organization and Party Democracy: The Emergence of the Cartel Party." *Party Politics* 1: 5–28.

Kristal, Tali. 2010. "Good Times, Bad Times: Postwar Labor's Share of National Income in Capitalist Democracies." *American Sociological Review* 75 (5): 729–63. doi: 10.1177/0003122410382640.

Lavoie, Marc and Engelbert Stockhammer. 2013. *Wage-Led Growth*. London: Palgrave.

Mosley, Layna. 2003. "Room to Move: International Financial Markets and National Welfare States." *International Organization* 54 (4): 737–73. doi:10.1162/002081800551352.

Onaran, Özlem and Giorgos Galanis. 2014. "Income Distribution and Growth: A Global Model." *Environment and Planning* A 46 (10): 2489–513.

Summers, Lawrence H. 2014. "U.S. Economic Prospects: Secular Stagnation, Hysteresis, and the Zero Lower Bound." *Business Economics* 4 (2): 65–73.

Tarantelli, Ezio. 1986. "The Regulation of Inflation and Unemployment." *Industrial Relations* 25 (1): 1–15.

CHAPTER 5

THE PHYSIOLOGY OF GREED

HERBERT A. REITSAMER

What drives people in the most diverse cultures to opt for a system of free-market economy? Are there common biological characteristics, stimulated by the basic mechanisms of capitalist development, that make it enjoyable for people to lay themselves open to this system?

Capitalism has become widespread throughout almost the entire world, and this raises the question of why, among other things, people seek to accumulate and increase capital, optimize profits, and steadily increase prosperity. Why are there often no upper limits that will make people permanently satisfied, and why does it seem that our excessiveness continues, even when we realize that this pursuit of more threatens our continued existence on this planet? The motivation behind our single-minded behavior must be deeply rooted within us, and for that reason, it may be interesting to take a look at the basic physiological mechanisms underlying our instinctive behavior.

Over the course of evolution, when it came to survival, humans, primates, and other creatures had very similar conditions and challenges to overcome. They were all equipped with a powerful drive to ensure the survival of the species, the group, and, especially, the individual. Thus, from the beginning, the main goals of our instincts were to ensure our reproduction and food supply. Our ancestors' dining tables were not as generously laden as they are today, and hunting and gathering did not succeed every day. Moreover, the early communities of primates, as well as all other living creatures, existed at the limits of survival most of the time. The group size of animal herds as well as the clans of our ancestors were evidently defined by the limited availability of food; the more successful their continuous procurement, the more extensively they were able to reproduce and spread. Greedy behavior was therefore important to ensure the survival of the individual and of the group.

In addition to our instinctive behavior concerning reproduction and food supply, there is also an organ— the gall bladder—that reminds us that we needed to be able to digest large amounts of fatty food in one go, that is, when hunting had been successful and no means of conserving food had yet been invented. Today, we need this organ only in a more limited way, as a continuous supply of food makes the release of large quantities of bile no longer necessary. Ironically, it is this same organ that tends to form stones in the case of diets comprising excessive animal fats and obesity (what we call diseases of affluence) and as a consequence must often be surgically removed.

Instinctive behavior is thus genetically predisposed and was set up as hardware in the phylogenetically old areas of our brain.

THE DIENCEPHALON

The diencephalon is where the important centers of our instincts, emotional processing, sensory functions, and other vital functions are located. This is where the body's autonomic functions have their morphological correlate—the sleep/wake cycle, sex drive, hunger and thirst, body temperature, and much more. It also provides the link between neuronal brain function and our hormonal system—for example, the translation of neuronal, mental arousal into the release of adrenaline, thyroid hormone, sex hormones, and cortisone.

We might imagine that demands on the control of our instincts have grown with the advance of civilization. However, this control takes place in a more modern part of our brain, the neocortex. While the old part of our brain stopped developing significantly over the course of evolution, a substantial development took place in the control region, the frontal neocortex. In evolutionary terms, it is the most recent part of our brain and one of the features that differentiate us fundamentally from other mammals. Although our instincts can be controlled much better than in less highly developed species, our diencephalon remains at the level of a frog sitting in a pool, waiting for an insect to appear within reach of its snapping mouth so that it can eat and so build the strength it needs to escape its enemies and continue its reproduction.

Nature has ensured that the actions leading to a successful fulfillment of the instincts are firmly anchored in the mind and are associated with a positive memory. So if the animal eats some food, it remembers where that took place and will visit the place again to try its luck once more. In humans, the same reward mechanisms exist as in less highly developed animals. They lead us to want to repeat positive stimuli, and ultimately very much want to give in to our instincts, even though we control them. For example, in a restaurant, we can suppress the urge to satisfy our desires until the waiter has served our particular meal. We do not fall upon our neighbors' food, because our parents have told us that such behavior is considered bad manners. But it is also possible that a memory from our childhood taught us that in the short term it was highly efficient, although not a good strategy, to steal the sandwich from a classmate. The negative consequences inflicted by the teacher, or possibly defeat in the subsequent fight, have been painfully lodged in our memory. The function of the prefrontal cortex and its significance for our social behavior, its ability to control spontaneous needs and to adapt instincts to the situation, becomes particularly clear when it is no longer functioning properly. This may be the case, for example, in conditions that arise as a result of injuries or circulatory disorders. People with a frontal lobe disorder may experience major personality changes, becoming uninhibited, childish, and impulsive. They give in to their instincts and lose the ability to judge suitable ways of behaving that are appropriate to the situation.[1]

THE REWARD SYSTEM

The reward system in our brain evaluates successful strategies positively and allows us to continue on the path to success throughout our lives. We like to keep acting according to this logic, because we are constantly rewarded for it. The reward comes in the form of the release of the neurotransmitter dopamine in the mesolimbic system, which forms part of the diencephalon and the limbic system. This release associated with other neurotransmitters (for example, oxytocin) brings us a feeling of well-being and a sense of satisfaction. The neuronal mechanism of reward was first investigated in rats. Two scientists, Peter Milner and James Olds, implanted microelectrodes in the brains of rats and placed them in Skinner boxes. The animals were able to move about freely, press a button, eat, and drink. On pressing the button, the animals triggered an electrical stimulation of the reward system in their brains. The stimulation produced a strong sense of reward and induced a rapid learning process, which very quickly led to the rats becoming addicted to this stimulation and pressing the button over and over again. This desire resulted in the animals not being able to fulfill even their most basic instinct—feeding—and they stopped eating and drinking because they preferred to stimulate their reward center by constantly pressing the button.[2] It also became clear that the reward mechanism lost its effectiveness with increasing duration and frequency. In order to achieve the same level of reward/satisfaction, the reward circuitry requires more and more input from the triggering stimuli. Drugs such as cocaine or amphetamines make use of this mechanism and lead to increased concentrations of dopamine in the synapses of the reward center, leading to an ever-increasing need for for the drugs, leading to addiction.

In addition to the current reward, positive gratifications of our intentions are also substantiated by positive memories. An associative learning process takes place in our brain, in which neurotransmitters such as serotonin and dopamine play a major role. This learning process means that even the anticipation of a positive stimulus leads to the release of neurotransmitters (particularly dopamine) in the brain.

It does not matter whether it is money or the enjoyment of sweet treats—with regard to the positive sensation that results from it, the brain's reward system is always involved. By now, it is clear that there are parallels between the reward mechanisms involved in drug use, eating, and gaming, and those associated with receiving money. It seems that any repetitive stimulus that is rewarded positively in the brain can potentially trigger a kind of addictive behavior. Repetitive reward, however, is subject to a deadening process, which can be attributed to the behavior of receptors in the synapses. As a result, the positive stimulus has to continually increase through repetitive stimulation, in order to achieve the same reward effect. However, individual susceptibility to both sensitization and the de-sensitization we have just described is very variable, and control as a result of experience and by the prefrontal cortex, as well as genetic predisposition, appear to play an important role.

However, the neuronal mechanisms of the reward systems that influence our daily actions are complex and cannot be reduced to a single circuit in the brain. For example, social comparisons can have modulating effects on our otherwise clear decisions. If a test subject in an experiment was offered two different sums of money, the person would usually opt for the higher sum. In a modified experiment[3] by Firebaugh and Tach,[4] test subjects were asked to choose one of two options. For doing the same job, a subject was offered an annual salary of $60,000 and was told that his colleague would receive $50,000. In the second option, the subject would earn $80,000, but his colleague would receive $90,000. Despite the higher salary in option two, the majority of subjects chose option one. Apparently, it was more important to them to fare better relative to their colleague, and so they rejected the higher income in favor of being better-off in social terms.

If the neuronal reward system and basic instincts can be found not only in humans but also in less highly developed species, we should be able to observe similar behaviors in the animal world as well. Simplified observations often make the animal world appear in an ideal light, where every animal only kills the prey that it needs to survive, and flora and fauna live in harmony. Although the latter may be true, this view clearly falls short. As long as there is enough prey, the hunter will, according to his basic instincts, try to satiate his hunger and reproduce—indeed, to the greatest possible extent. Through the reward system, he will learn where he can find the fattest prey, and will adjust his hunting methods accordingly. However, the ratio of hunter to prey is finely regulated. Lotka and Volterra developed a mathematical model that describes the dynamics of the hunter–prey system and enables the prediction of population development.[5] If the number of hunters increases too greatly, the number of prey species decreases and hunters can no longer find enough prey; the number of hunters then decreases and the prey population can recover.

Translated into human terms, this means that we encounter physical limitations in our accumulation of wealth. In this world, there simply exists no more land, gold, or other riches than what is physically available. Natural regulation through limited resources may take place. The road to virtual reality creates the possibility of the limitless growth of virtual assets without physical boundaries—a fact that should give our frog brain food for thought.

CONCLUSION

The brain's reward mechanism makes us pursue prosperity and accumulate riches. We can see greed for more as a relic of our phylogenetic development and as the burden or blessing of evolution. However, it must be clear to us in all our actions that, in a certain sense, we humans still act using our frog brain and that primitive, neuronal control circuits influence our decisions. Whether we spend or accumulate money, snack on sweet treats, or take stimulants, it is the reward circuit in the evolutionary old part of our brain that gives us a sense of well-being and seduces us into wanting to experience more and more of that positive feeling.

In conclusion, we can speculate whether capitalism found a good breeding ground in the evolutionary mechanisms that have ensured our survival in competition with natural forces and our natural enemies. We can take these considerations further and speculate that capitalism may have developed from precisely these archaic ways of behaving, and this is why it has spread so successfully.

Notes

1. https://www.cs.mcgill.ca/~rwest/wikispeedia/wpcd/wp/p/ Phineas_Gage.htm; https://de.wikipedia.org/wiki/Phineas_ Gage (both accessed December 4, 2018).

2. James Olds and Peter Milner, "Positive Reinforcement produced by Electrical Stimulation of Septal Area and other Regions of Rat Brain" in *Journal of Comparative and Physiological Psychology*, 47(6), 1954, pp. 419–427.

3. Glenn Firebaugh and Matthew B. Schroeder, "Does Your Neighbor's Income Affect Your Happiness?" in *American Journal of Sociology* (AJS), November 2009, 115(3), pp. 805–831.

4. Glenn Firebaugh and Laura Tach, "Relative Income and Happiness: Are Americans on a Hedonic Treadmill?" (session paper). https://www.eurekalert.org/pub_releases/2005-08/ asa-mcb080805.php (accessed December 4, 2018).

5. Alfred J. Lotka, *Elements of Physical Biology* (Baltimore, MD: Williams and Wilkins, 1925).

CHAPTER 6

GOD IS ALIVE, THE MARKET IS DEAD

BAZON BROCK

From the point of view of cultural studies, the debate about capitalism has been overly influenced by economics. This is astonishing since economics has conspicuously failed overall in both its predictions of and its retrospectively rationalizing explanations of, for example, recent financial crises—or has not been able or willing to offer convincing solutions. When Nobel Prize laureates in economic sciences applied their wisdom to economic activities it could only end in an extraordinary crash at the expense of their clients. So how can it be that the science of economics is still regarded as authoritative? Clearly, like the majority of all religions and theologies, it is based on people's need to respond to the dynamics of reality, that is to feel secure in their relationship with the world by interpreting it.

In their very assertion that they are based on economic data, the concepts traditionally used to celebrate or critique capitalism overlook the most important fact that it is above all counterfactuals that matter in society. The most significant fact is that all societies are subject to the normativity of the counterfactual.

Here's just one example: the owners of Middle Eastern oil wells have not used the billions and trillions of dollars paid to them by consumers to fall in line with the dominant requirements of Western capitalism. Instead, at every level they have tried to influence the spread of both Sunni and Shiite Islam by funding thousands of mosques and madrasas as well as nearly all the terrorists fighting for the absolute, propagating mass media of their own making, and suitably programmed networks supplied with military training. All this was and still is aimed quite legitimately at enforcing Sharia as an alternative to Western democracies with their rule of law and welfare systems.

Such procedures for legitimizing worldviews, religions, and ideologies are familiar from developments in the West. As an arch-capitalist society, the United

States takes succor from the belief that God's grace and protection is bestowed upon their system, and even that its representatives, as one of Goldman Sachs' chief executives has repeatedly and publicly emphasized, were helping to carry out God's divine plan through human means.

But capital is not second nature, that is an absolute spirit, independent of human needs like all the laws of nature; rather it is an important way of exercising power. Or, as smart people have said, capital is firepower for the exercise of power, especially market power. While economics can change these attributes merely by tweaking its image from *homo oeconomicus* to *homo psychologicus*, it remains ideology dressed up as science. At one time, this science was critical of what it called the "pseudo-sciences" of the Soviet Union, but it has now itself partly become what it once believed it could distinguish itself from. The political project known as "change through rapprochement" has actually come true; the West has completely adapted to the absolutism of the East because it believed it could easily assimilate it—but it was swallowed up. Over and over again in the course of history, the apparent victors turned into what they thought they had conquered. In the early 1990s, like most proponents of science as ideology, Francis

Fukuyama[1] was absolutely certain that the Western democracies and their fundamental capitalist principles would ultimately prevail over all competing systems. Today, with no shame or credible self-criticism, Fukuyama writes books stating the opposite of the prognoses he had previously developed scientifically.

The greatest danger to democracies, constitutional and welfare states, lies in the faith placed in science by politicians and other actors who take statements substantiated by scientific knowledge at face value—if it suits them. But as Karl Popper said, science can only be productive through critique, i.e. all the formulae offered by those who are apparently competent to provide solutions turn out to be illusory; because here on Earth, human problems can only be solved by creating new problems. The Pragmatic Sanction[2] states that alleged solutions to problems can be accepted as such, if the subsequent problems that arise individually during the course of the solution are smaller and hence more manageable than the initial problem. Such cases are indeed rare. In general, problems are considerable because they cannot be solved; if they were solvable, there would be no problem worthy of consideration, as Niklas Luhmann never tired of repeating the words of poor artists.

Science is no better acquainted with the truth than any other social system, but it can very well prove any ultimate justification to be false and thus help prevent them coming to fruition in a totalitarian environment.

Economists are all too inclined to regard capitalism as the ultimate justification for economic and thus social dynamics—and the Böckenförde dilemma[3] is an all too transparent fig leaf in this respect.

Since Marx's fundamental analysis, it has been customary to conceive of capitalism as the religion of modern societies. The god of capitalism as a religion is the market whose power is made manifest in capital. In turn, capital's impact on the market creates the Trinity of market, capital, and science/technology for devout consumerists. In science/technology, the spirit of the public realm appears as mediator between market and capital. In the temples of consumer culture, the cult of market and capital worship takes place in joyful submission. This submission prays for the longevity of that very consumer cult which promises to make offers of a reasonably enjoyable life available to all the least well-off at the lowest prices and for all eternity.

Agents of the media perform ritual and liturgy by celebrating this adoration of the exalted Trinity as a politically correct representation of diversity within the simple-minded unity of the ultimate justification after the alleged death of God. Everyone is entitled—as they are free to do—to participate in this cult, convinced of the certainty that they have the same life chances as everyone else. According to the incomparable definition, equal opportunities mean that all people have the same chance of picking six winning numbers in the national lottery.

And so God is alive and more powerful than ever, whether in the American or Islamic version of spirituality espoused by those who dominate the market, or just in the Trinity of market, capital, and spirit-as-public-realm in good old Western Europe. Just as Nietzsche believed he had to reveal the Christian teachings about Revelation as mere ideology by stating that "God is dead," so today capitalism is recognized as ideology in the equally self-assured statement "the market is dead." The offerings from lobbyists have blanketed the market, rendering it almost completely inefficient. Their tributes accompany their innumerable market interventions which are designed to make the market propitious to particular interests—exactly as the naively religious have tried since time immemorial to make God do their will by making offerings. "God is dead" was mere harmless speculation compared to today's announcement that the market is in danger of collapse. Three lobbyists per parliamentarian— representatives of market operators and thus also of devout consumers—prepare legal texts to optimize industry-specific profits by manipulating the markets. They see the laws of the market as a mere set of rules that can be shaped at will, just as they once believed they could conjure up the God they worshiped to suit their specific needs and pay homage to him. As means of countering this, the current antitrust legislation, the political framework within which capital operates in the financial sector and in the economy, or the prophylactic campaigns to raise social awareness in the market economy, as well as all the pious commitments to the primacy of education, are clearly as good as useless. As the Old Testament shows, the market, as the father of all creativity, creates the world through its spirit, not through *nomoi* (laws), or *deuteronomoi* (yet more laws). These laws are merely subsidiary forms of the primary process. The old debate about whether Jesus Christ was the same as God or like God—in Greek the debate over one *iota* (i),[4] which some people refuse to accept—turns up today in the debate about the question of whether capital itself defines the market (i.e. God merely in human form) or whether capital (formerly the Incarnate God) acts as a representative of the dynamics of the market (God the Father).

Shortly after the Emperor Constantine recognized Christianity as the true, victorious religion, faith leaders from AD 325 onwards developed a potent theology that is still unsurpassed in its intellectual power and persuasiveness. In the space of this short essay we cannot describe how this theology became the *mater studiorum*, i.e. the foundation of all the sciences and the arts, and thus of the power relations and social relations, which led to Europe's supremacy in the world, beginning in 1400. Christian theology achieved such importance in all its individual developments because at the highest scientific level it embraced one crucial social fact, namely the normativity of the counterfactual that governs all human relationships. Only the psychology of the late 19th century provided theology with serious competition. The sociology and economics of the mid-19th century missed their chance because they believed they could disregard the power of God as a ridiculous fairy tale compared with the might of machines and armies of workers. It took a very long time to show in terms of scientific theory that positivism was the very same ideology from which it so confidently believed it had to save humanity. In this tradition, we can include the broadening of the Nobel Prize disciplines to include economics, whose representatives owe much of their public reputation to the annual appointment of Nobel laureates. While particle physicists and their counterparts in cosmology have long understood that they owe their significance as human beings to their unparalleled affirmation as the modern theology of atheism, economists still cannot match this claim, even though they engage in mathematics with an almost childlike sense of creativity—mathematics being of course theology *par excellence*. Pure mental gymnastics exerts the greatest possible influence on the realities of human existence, as the *mathesis* genius Erwin Schrödinger showed.

So how do we save capitalism? On the one hand, by taking the market away from the capitalist lobby, as we once hoped and presently hope to be able to save faith, strengthened by doubt, from the domineering attitudes of the clerical aristocracy. We have never been capitalist, because the pure market that the capitalists invoke so emphatically precisely because they cannot allow it, has never existed.

On the other hand, we can save capitalism by using economics against pseudo-capitalism, just as powerful theology was once supposed to ward off the adulteration of the faith and prevented religious leaders from enhancing their status. An important way of doing this would be to replace mere forecasting with the Old Testament prophecy of anticipation. At its heart is the reversal of our current fixation on realism versus ideology: the concrete facts, factual givens, are seen as the result of historical evolution that is contingent, i.e. human-made, but nonetheless unchangeable (cf. *facta sunt servanda*). Nevertheless, the relationship of the contingent to its effect cannot be shown by how it arose, but rather by the counterfactual power of teleology. It is not factual genesis but counterfactual *telos* that determines the parameters within which both the individual and the collective act.

We can save capitalism by finally taking it seriously as a religion and endowing it with a suitable theology. Such an achievement might at last truly deserve a Nobel Prize in the theology of economics.

Notes

1. Francis Fukuyama, *The End of History and the Last Man* (New York: The Free Press, 1992).

2. In late antiquity, Roman law described the "Pragmatic Sanction" as a ceremonial legislative act by the emperor. The most famous example is the Pragmatic Sanction of 1713, a Habsburg law of succession issued by Emperor Charles VI.

3 "The liberal secular state lives by premises that it cannot itself guarantee. This is the great adventure it has undertaken for freedom's sake. As a liberal state it can only endure if the freedom it bestows on its citizens is regulated internally, both by the moral substance of individuals and the homogeneity of society. On the other hand, it cannot seek to guarantee these internal regulatory forces of its own accord, that is not through its own means such as legal constraint and authoritative decree. Doing so, it would surrender its liberal character and return, at a secular level, to the totalitarianism it once emerged from during the wars of religion." Ernst-Wolfgang Böckenförde, *Staat, Gesellschaft, Freiheit* (Berlin: Suhrkamp, 1976), p. 60.

4. Translator's note: When the early Church was considering the question of the nature of Christ, the language chosen had to be completely unambiguous—unlike "Son of God." In Greek, this debate drew a distinction between *homoousios* ("same being") and *homoiousios* ("like but not the same"), and thus the "i" or Greek letter *iota* made the crucial difference between two very similar words.

CHAPTER 7

ARE THE MARKET AND DEMOCRACY INTERDEPENDENT?

STEFAN KORIOTH

I.

For a long time after 1945 in the West and far beyond, democracy and the market economy went unchallenged. Today, both are in difficulties, even though since 1990 the alternative model of the socialist "people's democracy" with its planned economy has almost completely disappeared. In many countries, democracy is at the mercy of authoritarian temptations, which suggest that the pluralistic process's difficult but rewarding search for provisional solutions can be replaced by simple and unambiguous answers.[1] Even more strikingly, the market economy has been discredited. "The market" has been perceived as a threat to representative liberal democracies, and not just since the crisis years of 2008/09. To many people, the power of capital seems greater than that of the liberal social order. And, moreover, is it not forces aimed at unlimited growth that intensify both the waste of natural resources and social inequalities? In short, the destructive forces of the economic system seem to be a barrier to or even damaging to democracy. In 2008, shortly before the great crisis, a representative survey revealed that only 17 percent of citizens in the Federal Republic of Germany had a good opinion of the market economy.[2] In the social sciences beyond economics too, a critical view of capitalism[3] and the market seems to be intensifying for the first time since the 1960s. The sociologist Günter Dux sums it up:

> The modern understanding of the human form of existence expects the conditions for a self-determined way of life to be created as one that has purpose for everyone. This requires the social framework to be determined by this absolutely universal objective. But this proposition comes up against a market society whose economic system is determined by a partial rationale that runs categorically counter to the

universal proposition of the human form of existence. For, according to its systemic logic, the economic system pursues the interest of the owners of capital.[4]

So is there an inescapable conflict between the democratic and the economic system—on the one hand the self-determination of the few, on the other the ideal of self-determination for everyone? Or is it all completely different, with the system of market economy being a haven of freedom and prosperity for as many people as possible, in necessary symbiosis with liberal political forms? Perhaps it would help to pursue this question historically and empirically in the first instance (II.), and then to attempt a theory (III.).

II.

The market as an instrument for the allocation of scarce resources has always existed, while capitalist economic forms emerged at the beginning of the 19th century, boosted by technological revolutions, first in England, then in continental Europe and in the United States. This had little to do with democratic forms of political self-determination, although legal and economic theorists increasingly investigated questions concerning the interdependence between the state and economic systems. In practice, the crucial framework for the expansion of the capitalist system was "formal" equality and freedom for everyone (including before the law). Constitutionally, we talk about the formal rule of law, which was a huge step forward in the face of entrenched class inequality, but had the disadvantage of not taking into account the unequal early opportunities of individuals in society, which meant that sleeping under bridges at night was either prohibited or allowed in equal measure for everyone. This chimed with a state that was limited in its tasks and objectives, a state that erected no internal or external obstacles to economic expansion, and that handed both social welfare and redistribution over to private initiative. In the case of Germany in the second half of the 19th century, some historians even argue, unjustifiably, that economic freedom compensated for the lack of political freedoms.

The first half of the 20th century saw the decline of the market everywhere. In this respect, too, World War I led to the old world's descent into hell. In the USSR, a socialist model that shaped both state and economy, replacing freedom with control and duty, began to churn the economy rapidly through massive crises that culminated in famines. In Western countries, the transition to fully democratic forms of government was combined with new kinds of state intervention in the economy, most notably in Weimar Germany with its interventions and the introduction of elements of a redistributive welfare state financed by taxation. In the 1930s, following the Great Depression, the US proclaimed a "New Deal" that managed the economy through public investment, price and wage regulations, and demands for redistribution. All other major differences between the two states notwithstanding, a similar situation arose in National Socialist Germany. At almost the same time, the concept of the welfare state was born in Great Britain. After 1945, capitalism, the welfare state, and limited economic intervention were combined in the model of the social market economy, which could be seen most clearly in programmatic form in the federal state of West Germany,[5] and in Great Britain accompanied by occasional socialist features—confiscatory income tax and the nationalization of some key industries. Between 1950 and 1985 in all developed countries outside the socialist power bloc, public expenditure—government consumption as a share of total economic output—doubled. The end of the 1980s brought the next decisive change: a drastic withdrawal of the state took place—deregulation, privatization, and competition in as many areas of life as possible were the new guiding principles, which then were placed in doubt once again after 2008.

What can we deduce from the history of the link between democracy and the market? Nothing definitive, because the relationship is determined by many factors that do not reveal any clear trends. Nevertheless, and proceeding with all due caution, there is evidence that in the first place economic freedom and political freedom cannot be separated; and furthermore, in the second place, that democracies with universal and equal suffrage, at least from the outset, tend to regulate the economy and impose high taxes on economic activities. Their main objectives are to give the public sector the ability to act while at the same time reconciling the market and the state, balancing economic and social freedom. This option at the outset, however, is anything but lacking an alternative, as the East European democracies post 1990 show: initially, in the exuberance of expectations after the end of the planned economies and in light of the supposed end of history, democratic forms of government were combined with an unregulated economy.

The relationship between the market and democracy seems to go in waves—how else can we understand the marked turnaround in 1980s' politics towards neo-liberal forms of governance, which the then British Prime Minister Margaret Thatcher even accompanied with the deliberately provocative statement that there was no such thing as society, only individuals. These waves are the expression of a constant and complicated balancing of capital, market, and market economy on the one hand with the democratic political system on the other. Indeed, is it not the case that constant changes in this relationship are the very expression of a democratic system? Such re-balancings can be founded on objectives that have been changed democratically and are legitimate, but they can also take account of the economy's demands, which are injected into the democratic process or introduced into it under pressure. The democratic state, with its tendency to increase its scope and its considerable financial needs, uses its citizens' economic activities as a source of finance through taxation. In this respect, it lives as a "parasite" feeding off the private sector—to echo Schumpeter's famous formulation of 1918, when it was far from clear whether the future of the continental European states would lie in state socialism, state capitalism, or in the fundamental separation of economy and state. The democratic state itself depends on the existence of a functioning economic sector, which provides the necessary goods and services and finances state activities through its tax receipts.

Perhaps another assumption can be made: economic freedom requires political freedom, even if the fundamental conditions of economic freedom—protection of property, legal certainty, freedom of movement of goods and capital across borders—can be guaranteed in a variety of political systems. Whether the example of the People's Republic of China is moving towards this consecutive correlation between economic and political freedom remains to be seen. In any case, the combination of market economy (with numerous state enterprises) and socialist forms of government in China is a vast experiment that currently fills those in power with permanent distrust of their citizens. Not far from mainland China, the example of Taiwan demonstrates the attraction of economic freedom and increasing prosperity among large sections of the population. The link between capitalism and authoritarian forms of government, which was first established here after 1945, broke down in the early 1980s and, under considerable social pressure, the country transformed itself into a democracy with extensive constitutional safeguards. Economic freedom remained, but had to submit to stricter regulations. The example of Taiwan is also revealing in quite another way, however: in the process of democratization, the tax burden, public expenditure, and the national debt increased.

III.

The empirical evidence of the correlation between the market and democracy is thus by no means unambiguous. Certainly, there is a tendency for free markets to chime with free societies, and there are phases of successful social integration and social optimism that are sustained by economic success. On the other hand, there is the danger of overemphasizing the market, of society showing a one-sided appreciation of the individual's capacities for rational calculation, of competition, and of a whole range of financial incentives. Dutch economist Paul De Grauwe describes what this leads to:

> When the free market system grows in importance, as has been the case over the last three decades, these capacities in all individuals become more important. [...] However, that also means that other, equally important individual characteristics which belong to the emotional system [...] are suppressed. [...] For many people who care about fair income distribution, intrinsic motivation, and cooperation, this leads to a lack of fulfilment. The market system produces great material prosperity, but many people are dissatisfied all the same, because individual happiness is not achieved, or is even repressed. A discrepancy arises between individual and collective well-being, which can in

turn lead to the rejection of the system, which is felt to be hard, cold, and unfair. If this happens the social consensus in favor of the free market system is undermined.[6]

Starting from a different position, Thomas Piketty actually considers this to be unavoidable. It can be shown empirically, he writes, that the growth of capital exceeds the growth of the entire economy and thus promotes social inequality.[7] This contains an implicit assertion that democratic states are incapable of balancing labor and capital, thereby destroying the basis of their own legitimacy, in particular the promise of equality of justice.

Regardless of whether this is right or not, it cannot be denied that the relationship between the market and democracy is ambivalent. Economic and political freedom can be mutually supportive. However, free markets can also undermine the willingness to engage in fair, collective cooperation in the interests of the common good. In principle, economic freedom can also be protected by authoritarian regimes. The only question is whether this can succeed in the long run.

Thus it is perhaps not just the factors of freedom and self-determination that characterize successful markets and successful democracies, and the mutually beneficial relationship between market and democracy, as essential as these elements are. More important, perhaps, is the task and ability of a democracy to monitor the relationship between market and state, constantly maintaining its equilibrium in light of the political preferences of the majority. This prevents fluctuations in the direction of an exaggerated liberalization of markets, swings that might have to overestimate markets' ability to self-regulate, as well as the state's tendencies to control or take over the economy, through confiscatory taxes, overregulation, and nationalization, for example. In the words of De Grauwe: "Democracy helps." And, that should be understood as a normative measure:

> Democracy is needed to safeguard capitalism in the long term. Democratic institutions make it possible to identify collective interests quickly and give them a voice. This forces politicians to promote collective interests instead of the individual interests of the rich and influential. In this way democratic institutions bring stability. The discrepancy between collective and individual interests does not grow to excessive proportions.

But this means treading a fine line, as the example of the United States demonstrates: the US political system tends to favor the interests of the highest income groups.

This is closely related to the fact that in the US money is the determining factor in winning elections. To a certain extent it could be said that the US is also a victim of crony capitalism. That makes it very difficult for the government to take care of the public domain, such as the environment.[8]

Notes

1. Thomas Bauer's pamphlet, *Die Vereindeutigung der Welt* (Ditzingen: Reclam, 2018) even suggests that societies today are no longer prepared to tolerate diversity in all its manifestations.

2. Cf. Peter Bofinger, *Ist der Markt noch zu retten? Warum wir jetzt einen starken Staat brauchen* (Berlin: Econ, 2009), pp. 92f.

3. I use the word here not as a polemical battle cry, but to describe the form of economic activities that has dominated since the beginning of the 19th century.

4. Günter Dux, *Demokratie als Lebensform. Die Welt nach der Krise des Kapitalismus* (Weilerswist: Springer, 2013), p. 171.

5. The theory of "Ordoliberalism" (Walter Eucken/Franz Böhm) developed here was an explicit combination of market economics and democracy: the market and competition were inextricably linked to a constitutional state that protected personal autonomy and individual self-determination based on equal opportunities. The theory said that autonomy in the economic domain corresponded to a free political system. See Jochen Mohr, "Die Interdependenz der Ordnungen als rechts- und wirtschaftsphilosophische Konzeption" in *Juristenzeitung* 73 (2018), pp. 685ff.

6. Paul De Grauwe, *The Limits of the Market. The Pendulum between Government and Market,* trans. Anna Asbury (Oxford: Oxford University Press, 2017), pp. 53f.

7. Thomas Piketty, *Capital in the Twenty-First Century* (Cambridge, MA: The Belknap Press, 2014).

8. De Grauwe, *The Limits of the Market,* pp. 77f.

CHAPTER 8

DEMOCRACY AND THE MARKET ECONOMY—SOME THOUGHTS ON CHINA

MONIKA SCHNITZER

In the West, democracy and the market economy are two terms that are typically considered in conjunction with one another. For us, the market economy means that people are free to do business, that they are free to decide through what kind of work they earn their income, and what goods they buy with the income they earn. A central prerequisite for a functioning market economy is that people are able to rely on a functioning legal system in the context of their activities. In turn, political freedom is seen as guaranteeing that government provides this functioning legal system, while recognizing—in both senses of the word—the interests of its citizens. Freedom of expression and free elections ensure that people can articulate their needs and interests in relation to the state, and it is the job of political representatives to look after their constituents with regard to these needs.

For many decades in the planned economies behind the Iron Curtain and in China, these economic and political freedoms did not exist. In the 1980s, Gorbachev's reform policies in the Soviet Union began by addressing precisely these issues using *glasnost* [transparency] and *perestroika* [restructuring]. Freedom of speech and of the press were to be encouraged, preparations were made for the transition to a democratic system, and the economic system was to be restructured and geared towards features of a market economy.

At the same time, under Deng Xiaoping, China also began to open up to the West and to initiate a process of economic reform, and for many people in China, this raised their expectations that this process would also lead to new political freedoms. In my student hall of residence in London, this was also noticeable among the Chinese students, who, like me, were following developments in Eastern Europe and China in the summer of 1989 with great excitement. Their hopes were dashed in June 1989, when the student protests on Beijing's Tiananmen Square were violently quashed. Every night, they watched the television pictures broadcast on the BBC News with concern and bewilderment.

In the ensuing period, China's reform process led to unprecedented economic development, with average annual growth rates of around 10 percent. But despite the new economic freedoms and the enormous increase in the population's standard of living, barely thirty years after Tiananmen Square no democratization process has begun. Even the launch of the Internet and social media has changed nothing in this regard. Thus far, the government has successfully retained control of these channels of information and communication; and so far, the population, whose standard of living has continued to rise, seems to go along with it.

For Western observers this repeatedly raises the question: can this work in the long run? Can China continue to grow just as rapidly in the future as well? Surely economic development will some day reach its limits, if political freedoms are still not granted? In such an environment, can enough creativity emerge, not only to catch up with the technological standards of the West, but also to develop China's own cutting-edge technologies?

Let's take another look back at the start of China's transformation. In my lectures on the process of transformation in the planned economies, which I regularly gave at the end of the 1990s, I always focused on a comparison between the Chinese way and the Russian way. As research on the transformation processes showed, part of the success of China's reforms in the 1980s is actually due to the fact that the Communist Party granted economic freedoms without altogether relinquishing state control over the economy. The first reform measures stipulated that state-owned enterprises still had to fulfill their planned targets. Once this had been achieved, they could engage in economic activity at their own risk. This created incentives, but at the same time avoided destabilizing the existing system. Those who relied on low prices for everyday items in the old system were still guaranteed them. In Russia it was different. There, the centrally planned targets were no longer enforced during the transformation process. In the early phase of transformation, there was a significant decline in production and major social upheavals, putting further pressure on the political system.

But even after this first phase of the Chinese transformation, it could be seen that a strong government that does not have to take account of potential opposition from the people is much more capable of imposing and implementing large infrastructure projects. That is exactly what the Chinese government has been exploiting in the last few decades. For example, the expansion of the high-speed rail network has seen advances achieved in record time. This was also facilitated by the fact that the new network was not integrated into the existing rail network, but instead parallel structures were created. New stations were built and a completely new rail network was routed, running partially on piers high above the villages. Implementation in such a short period of time would be unimaginable in Western countries, given the approval procedures needed and taking into account the interests of those concerned. In comparison, the high-speed line between Nuremberg and Berlin was given the go-ahead in 1991, and the line opened in 2017. The distance of some 500 kilometers between Munich and Berlin can now be covered in four hours. Since the opening of the high-speed line in 2011 (after barely four years of construction), it takes five hours to travel the 1,300-kilometer distance between Shanghai and Beijing by train. For passengers this is a huge benefit, although the local population, whose houses lie beneath the new line, is probably less enthusiastic. In Germany, debates about the expansion of airports or about Stuttgart 21 illustrate the trade-off, which is between speed of implementation on the one hand and the population's political input on the other.

However, as previously indicated, the hitherto highly successful Chinese strategy, which relies on strong state control and foregoes the political participation of the population, may reach its limits when it comes to taking the next step in development. Up until now, China has focused mainly on importing Western capital and technological know-how into the country and producing goods for the global market as a production location with low labor costs. In view of the size of the market, Western companies have begun investing in China, even though they complained of a lack of legal certainty. Above all, the Chinese state's requirement that companies conduct research and development locally, in order to gain access to the Chinese market in the first place, worries Western companies operating there because of China's inadequate patent protection. In 2011, during a visit to China by the Commission of Experts for Research and Innovation set up by the German Federal Government, these topics were the focus of discussions with Western companies. At the same time, Western observers doubted that China would be able to develop its own innovative technologies and products for the foreseeable future, and the members of the Committee were also skeptical, as this requires innovative scientists, freedom, and creativity. How could these factors develop in a system that has few personal and political freedoms?

Just a few years later, it became apparent that this skepticism was misplaced. In fact, we can now see that China is no longer simply copying and imitating Western technologies and products, and that it no longer regards itself as an outposted workshop for Western companies. In recent years, China has caught up enormously in the field of research. The universities have expanded, and Chinese scientists trained in the West are being lured back home with lucrative offers.

The success of this expansion in research is reflected in the number of publications. In the last report of the Commission of Experts for Research and Innovation, the number of publications on the topic of "Autonomous Systems" was compared by individual country. In terms of the number of publications on this topic, China is on a par with Germany. In some branches, such as "Autonomous Systems in Industrial Production," China is even ahead of Germany in terms of the number of top publications.[1] A large increase in scientific publications in China, as recent studies show, can also be observed in the field of artificial intelligence. And the development of patents has also grown massively: there has been an increase not only in the overall number of patents, but also in the number of top patents with a particularly high degree of innovation. Thus the low level of democratization has not so far prevented China from catching up enormously in its research and development activities.

Remarkably, however, the huge increase in prosperity and the return of many overseas-trained scientists has not yet led to growing pressure for more political participation. In discussions with colleagues in China in the spring of 2017, the reason I was given for this was that people were significantly better off economically than just a few years ago, and that people were proud of this enormous economic development. Taken together, the palpable improvement in the individual's standard of living and the great pride taken in China's increasingly powerful role in the global economy characterize the attitude to life, as became clear during my conversations. So far, this seems to be enough to compensate for the lack of opportunities for political participation, and to hold society together. But will this remain so in the future?

The Indian economist and Nobel laureate Amartya Sen, who researches the relationship between freedom and economic development in developing countries, concludes that a country's economic development is an important precondition of freedom. It is only through this that people in poor regions have the opportunity of determining for themselves how they want to shape their lives; they have options and thus protection from exploitation by their employers, and this ultimately leads to the prospect of political freedom. Looked at in this way, we can see China's enormous growth as a necessary step towards more freedom, even political freedom, for the population.

In promoting further economic development, however, a reliable constitutional state, as mentioned earlier, plays a central role. Those who want to grow their potential in an unfettered way must be able to depend on the protection of property and the adherence to contracts; they must be able to rely on free competition and be secured against monopolizing tendencies from (possibly state-sponsored) competitors; and they must be protected from arbitrary interference and encroachments by the state and from corruption. Without a political voice, it is hard to imagine that this legal certainty can be guaranteed. Equally, a state that the people no longer trust to act in their interests will pay for this with a decline in economic momentum. Whether the people will remain politically reticent if growth rates decline and scope for the distribution of wealth diminishes, remains open to question.

Note

1. EFI – Commission of Experts for Research and Innovation, *2018 Report on Research, Innovation, and Technological Performance in Germany*, Chapter 3 (Berlin: EFI, 2018).

CHAPTER 9

THE RISE OF CHINA AND ITS IMPLICATIONS FOR THE WORLD

JUSTIN YIFU LIN

This year China is celebrating the 40th anniversary of her transition from a planned economy to a market economy. The country's economic performance since the transition started has been a miracle of human history. In 1978 China was one the poorest countries in the world, her per capita GDP was $156, less than one third of the average of $490 in Sub-Saharan African countries. Like other poor countries, 82 percent of her population was living in rural areas and 84 percent of her population was living below the international poverty line of $1.25 a day. China was also an inward-looking economy with trade consisting of merely 9.7 percent of her GDP. From this humble starting point, China achieved an average annual GDP growth rate of 9.5 percent and trade growth rate of 14.8 percent during the period 1978–2017. China became the second largest world economy, measured in the market exchange rate, in 2009 by overtaking Japan; the largest exporter in the world in 2010 by overtaking Germany; the largest trading country in the world in 2013 by overtaking the USA; and the largest economy in the world, measured in purchasing power parity, in 2014 by overtaking the USA. More than 700 million people have been lifted out of poverty, contributing to more than 70 percent of the global poverty reduction in this period. Moreover, China is the only emerging market economy in the world that did not suffer from a homegrown financial crisis. In 2017 China's per capita GDP reached $8,640. It is most likely that China will cross the threshold of $12,700 and become a high-income economy around 2025. If the above prediction comes true, China will be the third country, following South Korea and Taiwan among nearly 200 developing economies, to successfully grow after World War II from low income to high income.

In this essay, drawing on Lin,[1] I would like to discuss why it was possible for China to achieve such an outstanding performance after the transition in 1978; why it was impossible to have a similar performance before 1978; why there have been repeated predictions about the coming collapse of the Chinese economy in the past decades in spite of China's superb stability and dynamic growth; what prices China paid for her success; and lastly what lessons the world can learn from China's transition success.

1. WHY CHINA GREW SO RAPIDLY AFTER 1978

A continuous stream of technological innovation in the existing industries and the emergence of higher value-added industries is the basis for continuous improvement in productivity and income and thus sustained growth in any economy, for both high-income and developing countries.

There are, however, some important differences between advanced high-income countries and developing countries. In advanced high-income countries, technologies and industries are already at global technological frontiers. To upgrade, they have to invent new technologies and industries to move these frontiers forward. Invention requires huge capital expenditures and is also very risky. From the end of the 19th century until today, the average annual growth rate of per capita labor productivity and per capita GDP in high-income countries were about 2 percent per year, and their annual GDP growth rate for the whole nation was about 3 percent to 3.5 percent.

For developing countries, their technologies and industries are within global technological and industrial frontiers. They can acquire or imitate technologies and industries from high-income countries to achieve technological innovations and industrial upgrading. In this way, technological innovations and industrial upgrading in developing countries will have lower costs and risks than in advanced high-income countries. This possibility is the so-called latecomer advantage or advantage of backwardness.[2] If developing countries are able to tap into that advantage, they can achieve higher rates of technological innovation and industrial upgrading, and thus have a fast rate of growth, a fast rate of improvement in labor productivity, and growth in income.

Since World War II, 13 economies in the world have found a way to realize the potential of latecomer's advantage and achieve average annual GDP growth rates of 7 percent or over for 25 or more years.[3] A growth rate of 7 percent or over was therefore more than twice that of high-income countries. If this rate is sustained for 25 or more years, the gap between the country concerned and high-income countries will decline. China became one of these 13 economies after the transition started in 1978.

2. WHY CHINA FAILED TO GROW DYNAMICALLY BEFORE 1978

If the latecomer's advantage is the secret for China's success over the past 40 years, why did China fail to benefit from that potential and achieve dynamic growth before the transition to a market economy in 1978, when that advantage had been available for centuries? This failure was because China adopted a wrong development strategy after the socialist revolution in 1949.

Mao Zedong and other first-generation revolutionary leaders in China, like many revolutionary leaders in other developing countries, were inspired by the dream of achieving rapid industrialization and modernization. The lack of large scale, advanced, capital-intensive, heavy industries that were the basis of military strength and economic power was perceived as the root cause of the country's backwardness. It was natural for the social and political elites in China to prioritize the development of large, heavy, advanced industries after the Revolution as they began to build the nation. Starting in 1953, China adopted a series of ambitious Five-Year Plans to accelerate the building of modern, advanced industries, with the goal of overtaking Britain in ten years and catching up with the United States in 15 years. But China was a lower-income, agrarian economy at that time. The country did not have comparative advantages in terms of modern, advanced industries, and Chinese firms in those industries were not viable in an open, competitive market.

To achieve its strategic goal, the Chinese government needed to protect its priority industries by giving firms in those sectors a monopoly and subsidizing them through various price distortions, including suppressed interest rates, an overvalued exchange rate, and lower prices for inputs. The price distortions created shortages and the government was obliged to use administrative measures to mobilize and allocate resources directly to nonviable firms.[4]

These interventions enabled China to quickly establish modern advanced industries, test nuclear bombs in the 1960s, and launch satellites in the 1970s. But the resources were misallocated, the incentives were distorted, and the labor-intensive sectors in which China had a comparative advantage were repressed.

As a result, economic efficiency was low, growth was driven mainly by an increase in inputs, and people were poor.

3. WHY THERE WERE REPEATED PREDICTIONS ABOUT THE COLLAPSE OF THE CHINESE ECONOMY

Repeated predictions about the imminent collapse of the Chinese economy emerged because China did not follow the mainstream Washington Consensus recipe advocated in the West for her transition.

After World War II, all the socialist countries and most other developing countries, guided by the prevailing structuralism, also adopted a similar strategy and government interventions to accelerate the development of advanced, capital-intensive industries on the basis of a capital-scarce economy, and had a poor economic performance similar to that of China. When China started the transition from a planned to a market economy, many other socialist and developing countries embarked on a similar transition as well. In the 1980s and the 1990s, the dominant neoliberalism in the West regarded the government failure arising from excessive government interventions as the root cause of poor economic performance in the socialist and other developing countries. It recommended a shock therapy to implement the Washington Consensus package of privatization, marketization, and stabilization for the transition to a market economy, which was the consensus among leading economists in the world at that time.[5] China did not follow this shock therapy. Instead, China adopted a pragmatic, gradual, piecemeal, dual-track approach for her transition, providing transitory protection and subsidies to the state-owned enterprises in the existing capital-industries and simultaneously liberalizing and facilitating entry into new labor-intensive and small-scale traditional industries, which were consistent with China's comparative advantages. This piecemeal approach was considered the worst possible transition strategy, doomed to cause more rent-seeking as well as corruption and worse misallocation of resources than before.[6] Therefore, once the growth in China decelerated, the prediction of China's coming collapse surged in both the press and the global academic community. However, in those countries that adopted the shock therapy recommended by the neoliberal Washington Consensus, their economies collapsed, stagnated, and were hit by frequent crises after their transition. Their economic performance in the 1980s and 1990s was worse than it had been in the 1960s and 1970s.[7] China maintained dynamic growth and was the only emerging market economy without a homegrown crisis in the past 40 years.

The contrasting performance between China and other transition economies is because the neoliberal recipe failed to recognize that the purpose of those distortions before the transition was to protect the comparative advantage-defying, large-scale, capital-intensive industries. If the government eliminated those distortions immediately, these large-scale industries would go bankrupt and a large number of workers would lose their jobs, undermining social and political stability. Without social and political stability, economic development is impossible. As a result, after the Washington Consensus shock-therapy reform, many countries reintroduced subsidies and protection in order to preserve jobs.

Moreover, many of these large-scale industries were defense-related. Even after privatization, governments continued to subsidize them to keep them in operation. As a result, whether it was for reasons of social stability or national defense, after privatization, liberalization, and marketization, the government reintroduced new types of subsidies and distortions. These distortions were even more inappropriate and even more inefficient than the explicit subsidies and protections that had been swept away.

Before privatization, the managers were state employees. If there were difficulties, they would ask the government for protection and subsidies. If the government were to provide assistance, the managers could at most increase their on-the-job consumption. Putting money into their own pockets, however, was corruption and punishable. After privatization, owners of those large enterprises also asked for subsidies. In this case, subsidies could simply be turned into their own wealth, and there was an incentive for asking for yet higher subsidies and assistance. As a result, reform led first to chaos followed by stagnation and frequent crises.

Retrospectively, the pragmatic, dual-track approach was a better approach than shock therapy. The transitory protection and subsidies to the existing sectors helped China maintain stability. The government's liberalization and facilitation of entry into the traditional, labor-intensive industries helped China grow dynamically. In the past, the government discriminated and repressed these labor-intensive sectors. To make such industries transform comparative advantage into competitive advantage, China also needed to provide adequate infrastructure and a good business environment. The infrastructure in China was extremely poor when the transition started. Although it was desirable to improve infrastructure for the whole nation, the Chinese government lacked the financial resources to do so, and so it set up special economic zones (SEZs), industrial parks, and export-processing zones, improving infrastructure in a limited number of areas. China's business environment was also very poor due to the distortions needed to protect existing industries. In SEZs and other economic zones, however, the government eliminated all of these distortions. In addition, the government provided a one-stop service and other incentives to the firms in SEZs or industrial parks. As a result, new industries consistent with China's comparative advantage quickly became China's competitive advantage.

It was for these reasons that China maintained stability, achieved dynamic growth, and China's exports rose rapidly in the last four decades. As China grew and accumulated capital, China's comparative advantages gradually upgraded from labor-intensive to capital-intensive industries. During the upgrading process, China was able to benefit from the latecomer's advantage.

4. THE PRICE CHINA PAID FOR HER SUCCESS

Although the economic performance during the transition in the last four decades was extraordinary, China also paid a very high price for her success. In addition to environmental degradation and food safety issues, which drew many public complaints and were the results of rapid industrialization and lack of appropriate regulations, the main issue during the transition was widespread corruption and worsening of income disparities as predicted by economists against a gradual transition approach. Before 1978, China had a more disciplined and clean bureaucratic system and an egalitarian society. According to the Corruption Perception Index published by Transparency International, China ranked 79 out of all 176 countries or territories in 2016; and based on the estimates of the National Statistical Bureau and various scholars' research, after 2000 China's Gini coefficient has exceeded 0.45, higher than the international warning level.[8] These problems were related to China's pragmatic, dual-track transition strategy.

As already mentioned, the Chinese government adopted a pragmatic, dual-track approach in the transition. On the one hand, the government provided transitory protection and subsidies to the nonviable state-owned enterprises in the old, capital-intensive sectors to maintain stability and, on the other hand, liberalized and facilitated entry to the new, labor-intensive sectors which were consistent with China's comparative advantages to achieve dynamic growth. One of the most important costs of investment and operation for the old capital-intensive sectors was the cost of capital. Before the transition in 1978, the government used fiscal appropriation to pay for investments and cover working capital: the SOEs did not have to bear any capital costs. After the transition, the fiscal appropriation was replaced by bank loans. The Chinese government set up four large state banks and a stock market to meet the capital needs of large enterprises. To subsidize the SOEs, interest rates and capital costs were artificially suppressed.

When the transition started, almost all firms in China were state-owned. With the dual-track transition, private-owned firms grew and some of them became large enough to get access to bank loans or be listed on the equity market. As interest rates and capital costs were artificially suppressed, anyone who could borrow from the banks or be listed on the stock market was therefore subsidized. These subsidies were paid for by the low returns to savings made by individual households in the banks or on the stock market.

Those people providing the funds were poorer than the owners of the large firms they financed. Subsidizing the operation of rich people's firms by poorer people was one reason for increasing income disparities. Moreover, the access to bank loans and the equity market generates rents, leading to bribery and corruption of the officials who control access.

Similarly, before 1979 mining for natural resources was operated free of concession fees by large-scale, state-owned mining companies, and the outputs were provided to other state-owned enterprises at very low prices. The government allowed private firms to enter the mining sectors in 1983 and liberalized controls over output prices in 1993. Concession fees and output taxes were kept low as a measure to compensate for state-owned mining enterprises' social policy burden of employing redundant workers and covering the pensions of retired workers.[9] For new private mining companies, they do not have those social policy burdens. Acquiring a concession promises them wealth overnight and becomes a source of income inequality and corruption.

In addition, some natural monopoly industries, such as power and telecommunications, are operated by state-owned enterprises. The government liberalizes the entry to those industries gradually. These monopoly rents are also sources of inequality and corruption.

To deal with the corruption issue, President Xi Jinping launched an antigraft campaign after taking office in 2013. However, the root of widespread corruption was the rents arising from the distortions embodied in the dual-track transition for the purpose of protecting and subsidizing the large-scale SOEs in comparative-advantage defying, capital-intensive industries. In the 1980s and 1990s China was a poor country and capital was scarce. After four decades of rapid economic growth, capital became relatively abundant and China's comparative advantages evolved accordingly. Many capital-intensive industries turned from defying China's comparative advantages to becoming consistent with China's comparative advantages. As a result, firms in those industries became viable and should have been competitive and profitable in domestic and global markets as long as they had good management. The nature of subsidies and protections to the recipient firms changed from a necessity for survival to a pure rent. It is imperative and high time that all remaining distortions and protections were eliminated so as to complete the transition to a well-functioning market economy and to root out the causes of corruption and income disparity. Indeed, this is precisely the intention of the comprehensive reform agenda adopted in 2013 by the third plenary session of the 18th Party Congress of Communist Party of China.

5. WHAT ARE THE LESSONS FOR OTHER DEVELOPING COUNTRIES AND FOR ECONOMICS?

What, finally, are the implications for other developing countries? The analysis in this paper suggests, first, that every developing country has the potential to grow dynamically and continuously for 30 years or more, and to eliminate poverty and become prosperous if they develop their economies according to their comparative advantage. With government facilitation in a market economy, countries can turn their comparative advantages into competitive advantages. Competitive industries can be profitable, accumulate capital, and engage in processes of industrial upgrading that tap into the potential advantage of backwardness, enabling them to grow much faster than high-income countries, maintaining growth rates of 7 percent or more for several decades, as has been the case in China over the last four decades. If they can realize this growth potential, the United Nations' 17 Sustainable

Development Goals to be achieved by all countries in the world by 2030 can be realized. Prosperity and job opportunities in developing countries will reduce illegal migration and refugees and contribute to world peace. Although the potential is there for every country to grow, they need to have the right development strategy in order to tap into the potential.

Second, most countries inherit many distortions from previous interventions. These distortions cause the misallocation of resources and rent-seeking. Removing those distortions are desirable. However, distortions exist for certain reasons, and are, in economic terms, largely endogenous. Unless the causes of a distortion are removed first, the attempt to eliminate the distortion can do more harm than good. A country embarking on reform should therefore be pragmatic, employing transitory and transitional protection as China has done over the last 30 years.

A careful liberalization of entry into new sectors consistent with a country's comparative advantages and government facilitation of growth in those sectors can allow it to grow dynamically and preserve stability, while preparing the ground for the removal of distortions. A pragmatic approach to step-by-step development according to a country's evolving comparative advantage is of great value for developing countries.

At the same time, pragmatism is required in the transition itself. The final goal is the establishment of a well-functioning market economy, but it should be a process managed by the government paying attention to the needs of all sectors and providing business opportunities for them.

The analysis in this paper shows that it is important to examine the reality of the situation in the developing countries and to develop new ideas and theoretical understandings based on their experiences. In recent years, reflecting on the weakness of structuralism and neo-liberalism, I have advocated the new structural economics as the third generation of development economics,[10] which is generalized from the success and failure of China and other developing countries' development and transition. From the perspective of new structural economics, the secret of China's success is her use of both the "invisible hand" and "visible hand," forming an organic integration, complementation, and mutual improvement of the functions of the market and the state. The applicability of a theory that is generalized from one country to other countries depends on the similarity of pre-conditions in the country and other countries. I hope that the new structural economics will provide useful insights for developing countries

as they overcome development challenges on the
roads ahead.

Notes

1   Justin Yifu Lin, *Demystifying the Chinese Economy*
    (Cambridge, UK: Cambridge University Press, 2012).

2   A. Gerschenkron, *Economic Backwardness in Historical
    Perspective: A Book of Essays* (Cambridge, MA: Belknap Press
    of Harvard University Press, 1962).

3   World Bank (on behalf Commission on Growth and
    Development), *The Growth Report: Strategies for Sustained
    Growth and Inclusive Development* (Washington, DC: World
    Bank, 2008).

4   Justin Yifu Lin, *Economic Development and Transition:
    Thought, Strategy, and Viability* (Cambridge, UK: Cambridge
    University Press, 2009).

5   Larry Summers, "Comment." In *The Transition in Eastern
    Europe*, edited by Oliver Jean Blanchard, Kenneth A. Froot,
    and Jeffrey Sachs, vol. 1, 252–253. (Chicago, IL: Chicago
    University Press,1994).

6   K. Murphy, A. Schleifer, and R.W. Vishny, "The Tradition
    to a Market Economy: Pitfall of Partial Reform" *Quarterly
    Journal of Economics* 107: 889–906 (1992).

7   William Easterly, "The Lost Decades: Developing Countries'
    Stagnation in Spite of Policy Reform 1980–1998." *Journal of
    Economic Growth* 6: 135–157 (2001).

8   S. Li and T. Sicular, "The Distribution of Household Income
    in China: Inequality, Poverty and Policies." *China Quarterly*
    217: 1–41 (2014).

9 Justin Yifu Lin and Guofu Tan, "Policy Burdens, Accountability, and the Soft Budget Constraint." *American Economic Review: Papers and Proceedings* 89: 426–431 (1999).

10 Justin Yifu Lin, *New Structural Economics: A Framework for Rethinking Development and Policy* (Washington, DC: World Bank, 2012).

CHAPTER 10

THE CHINA CHALLENGE—A
BUSINESS PERSPECTIVE

STEFAN OSCHMANN

Thinking about the future of capitalism or market
economics today primarily means thinking about
China. It is only a matter of time until the People's
Republic overtakes the United States as the world's
largest economy. China has already been a major political and economic force for a long time now. And the
country is making major advances in science and technology. Today, we in the Western world agree that the
decisions made by the leadership in Beijing have geopolitical consequences and that they shape the markets
and the rules of the game in international economic

relations. In the future, however, the major Chinese digital groups and many of the scientists and entrepreneurs in Beijing, Shanghai, Guangzhou, and other Chinese cities will play a decisive role in shaping our world. The future of capitalism will largely be defined in the People's Republic of China. This is not entirely without irony given that the ruling Communist Party is officially committed to Marxism and the "socialist market economy." We should set such bold concepts aside, however, and take a sober look at the facts.

A BREATHTAKING RESURGENCE

From a historical point of view, no other economic system has enabled as much human progress as the market economy. The market economy stimulates human creativity and unleashes dynamic economic activity, thus leading to increasing prosperity. Clearly, a functioning market economy requires good regulations and responsible entrepreneurs. With the right framework, it can enable great human progress—as shown not least of all by China's breathtaking economic climb over the last four decades.

Actually, we should call it a resurgence. For many centuries, China was the most important country on earth in economic terms. Many technological innovations were developed here, such as paper, the compass, and gunpowder. Only with the Opium War of 1840 did a political and economic decline begin. In the following decades, the country suffered under colonial powers, occupiers, a long civil war, and the rule of Mao Zedong. The turning point came only 40 years ago, under the leadership of Deng Xiaoping. His policy of opening up the country marked the start of one of humanity's greatest economic success stories. For many years, the Chinese economy achieved double-digit growth rates. More than 600 million people escaped poverty. Today, there are well over 100 million Chinese households with disposable annual incomes of more than US$21,000; by comparison, the figure was only two million households in the year 2000.

More than almost any other country, China has profited from the economic globalization of recent years. From 2000 to 2016, Chinese exports rose more than eightfold, from around US$250 billion to US$2.1 trillion.[1] Today, China is Germany's largest trading partner by sales[2] and the European Union's second largest.[3]

There is no doubt about it, China's economic resurgence is breathtaking, just like the economic and socio-political challenges that the country still faces.

THE ECONOMIC CHALLENGES ARE STILL GREAT

With around 1.4 billion inhabitants, or a good fifth of the world's population, China, despite all its economic successes, still faces major social challenges. Many hundreds of millions still live in poverty; around half of the population lives on less than US$5.50 per day. And, at the same time, the high growth rates of recent years seem to have finally come to an end. As recently as 2010, the Chinese economy achieved an annual growth rate of 10.6 percent. In 2017, the growth rate was 6.9 percent; for 2018 the IMF is forecasting only 6.6 percent, and for 2019 6.2 percent. In addition, rising wages are causing China's price competitiveness with regard to simple production activities to decline, for example in comparison to its Southeast Asian neighbors. At the same time, in terms of productivity and automation, the country lags considerably behind established industrialized nations such as Germany and the United States.

The Chinese government has recognized these challenges and the potentially explosive social tensions inherent in them, and has initiated a fundamental change of course in economic policy.

THE GOVERNMENT SETS THE COURSE

China's economy has little in common with the Soviet-style planned economies. Yet the party's guidance still has a decisive impact on the development of the "socialist market economy." What we see here is not a market economy in the classic Western sense. In China, investment decisions must invariably take political priorities into account; they are not made solely on the basis of economic criteria.

A fundamental tool which the government uses to shape economic developments is its five-year plans. With its 13th and current five-year plan, covering the period from 2016 to 2021, China aims to develop into a "moderately prosperous society."[4] Core elements of the plan include strengthening innovative technologies, accelerating urbanization, reforming the health sector, and ensuring better protection for the environment.

To maintain growth, the government is changing course—away from cheap production and towards an innovation-driven economy. To this end, the government is making targeted investments in the fields of science and technology. Since 1999, China's investments in research and development have increased by around 20 percent per year[5] and currently amount to more than US$230 billion, or around 20 percent of total R&D spending worldwide.[6] Nowhere are there more university graduates with degrees in the natural sciences and engineering. The goal is clear: the country aims to transition from "the world's workbench" to a global innovation leader. The Chinese government is thus pursuing a rigorous industrial policy and has initiated a number of strategies and programs. They address a very wide range of different topics and policy areas, but together they form a coherent package of measures aimed at strengthening the Chinese economy in the long term and consolidating the country's status as a leading global economic power.

MADE IN CHINA 2025

One key measure is the "Made in China 2025" strategy, which the Chinese government announced in 2015. This master plan was influenced by international role models such as the "Industry 4.0" concept in Germany and the "Industrial Internet" in the United States. By 2025, the Chinese leadership aims to have significantly modernized the country's industrial infrastructure and to have developed domestic high-tech industries. Plans call for increased expenditures for research and development, increased use of digital production technologies, a significant reduction in CO_2 emissions, and other measures over the coming years.

The time horizon for "Made in China 2025" stretches far beyond the stated target year. By 2035, China aims to compete with the world's industrialized nations on an equal footing. And by 2045, the country aims to itself be a leading global industrial location. This goal is to be achieved by focusing on innovation-driven production, high quality standards, environmental sustainability, and good education. "Made in China 2025" identifies ten strategically important technologies that contribute around 40 percent of economic output, including energy-efficient vehicles, innovative drugs, and new materials. On balance, the master plan can be expected to lead to greater demand for cutting-edge technologies on the part of Chinese companies. At the same time, however, Chinese high-tech companies will themselves be entering the international markets on a broader basis than before. If the Chinese leadership consistently implements "Made in China 2025," then, in a few years, the country can indeed be expected to rank among the leading locations for research and development and high-tech production.

HEALTHY CHINA

Improving healthcare is a further priority of the Chinese government. The People's Republic has made major advances in this area in recent years, as a look at life expectancy shows. In 1978, the year in which the country began to open up economically, life expectancy was just under 66 years. Until 2016, it rose continuously, and has meanwhile increased to more than 76 years.[7] That is already close to the European level. For comparison: in Germany, life expectancy at birth in 2016 was just under 81 years.

In the meantime, almost all Chinese people have health insurance. In comparison with established industrialized nations such as the United States or Germany, however, the share of health expenditures in GDP is still very low, at 6 percent.

Moreover, the country suffers from an unfavorable demographic trend. The number of people over the age of 65 will increase significantly in coming years, both in absolute terms and as a ratio to young people, as the birth rate remains low despite the termination of the one-child policy.

With the "Healthy China 2030" strategy, the government aims to significantly improve health-care for the Chinese population. In roughly 12 years, the country aims to reach a level comparable to that of the industrialized nations. The key aspects of "Healthy China 2030" are the promotion of healthier lifestyles, better monitoring of key risk factors, a healthier environment, and access to basic healthcare for all citizens. Moreover, the government aims to further optimize and expand the healthcare sector. One concrete example is that the current doctor density of 2.2 physicians per 1,000 inhabitants is to rise to three physicians per 1,000 inhabitants.

Another important goal is the expansion of research and development in the area of innovative drugs. Expenditures in this area are rising much faster in China compared to the global average. Today, China is already the second-largest pharmaceutical market worldwide and, in a global comparison, it is growing the fastest. In this context, it will also be important for the government to accelerate review and regulatory approval processes, adjust local standards to reflect global standards, and better protect intellectual property. Following this course, Chinese pharmaceutical companies can indeed be expected to soon rank among the leading companies in their sector worldwide. At the same time, major growth opportunities are opening up for international companies; increasingly, they could bring not only generics and almost identical copies of biologic medicines (biosimilars) to the Chinese market, but innovative medicines as well.

STRATEGIC DEVELOPMENT OF A DIGITAL ECOSYSTEM

In regard to the digital economy, today China indisputably holds second place behind the United States. Of the 20 leading Internet companies, nine are Chinese and eleven are American. The best-known among the Chinese firms are doubtless Baidu, Alibaba, and Tencent, often also known as BAT. They are the dominant companies of the digital ecosystem in China. They are profiting from the government's policy of largely blocking the US groups, which are the global leaders, from entering China by means of the "Great Firewall." In the long term, however, these companies will not be satisfied with merely serving the Chinese market. In the foreseeable future, the Chinese platforms will increasingly enter international markets themselves.

Today, China is a key driver of digital progress. In 2017, venture capital investments in the country totaled US$65 billion dollars.[8] For comparison: in the United States, the figure was US$84 billion,[9] in the European Union only US$19 billion.[10]

A major share of this venture capital goes to artificial intelligence. In 2017 the Chinese government set the goal of becoming one of the global leaders in this area by 2030. At present, in the field of AI alone, 14 Chinese start-ups have reached "unicorn" status, or in other words a market value of more than US$1 billion.[11] As this example shows, technologies are currently emerging in China that are significant in terms of global economic development. Chinese scientists and entrepreneurs are creating important platforms for the global economy of tomorrow.

BELT AND ROAD

Hardly any Chinese government project has garnered as much attention in recent years as the "Belt and Road" initiative. It was first announced in September 2013 in Kazakhstan by head of state and party leader Xi Jinping. This ambitious plan calls for expansion and development of the land and sea routes connecting China with numerous countries of Asia, Africa, and Europe. It includes, among other things, the expansion of transit routes from western China through Pakistan to the Arabian Sea (the "China-Pakistan Economic Corridor"), train connections extending all the way to

Western Europe, and port facilities in countries such as Sri Lanka and Djibouti. With this project, China will open up new trade routes and markets and ensure its access to key raw materials, and in addition, it will strengthen its economic ties to these countries, which account for almost two-thirds of the world's population. Naturally, the country gains geopolitical influence in this way as well. With the "Belt and Road" initiative, the People's Republic is enhancing its international standing and strengthening its position as a key center of gravity in a multi-polar world.

TRADE POLICY

China's government has a stated commitment to an open trade policy. Today the country is strongly integrated in global value-added chains, no longer solely as a production location, but also in the area of research and development and, of course, as an important sales market. President Xi's support for further opening the country and reducing customs barriers, which he expressed at the Boao Forum for Asia in Hainan in southern China, is thus a very welcome development. The announcement regarding better enforceability of intellectual property rights sends an important signal to international companies as well. The important thing now is to make significant progress in these areas.

Overall, China has managed very well so far with its politically guided, centrally planned market economy. Millions of people have been freed from the most bitter poverty. Naturally, economic growth on this scale is not achieved without setbacks and risks. The possible escalation of the trade dispute with the United States, and the at times very high public debt,[12] pose risks for the country's future growth. Despite all the challenges which lie ahead, however, the country is well on its way to becoming one of the global leading industrialized nations.

A HIGHLY DYNAMIC MARKET

An economy the size of China's, with 1.4 billion people, naturally cannot be exclusively centrally planned. Chinese society is very complex, and it is developing very rapidly. For international companies, it is essential to take the preferences of Chinese consumers into account. Car manufacturers, therefore, put other models on the market in the People's Republic, for example, and sweets manufacturers adapt the flavors of their products to meet local tastes. New technologies spread very rapidly in China. E-commerce plays a much more important role than in Europe or the United States. A few figures paint an impressive picture: while in the United States, the so-called "Black Friday" after the Thanksgiving holiday in 2017 saw US$2.4 billion in sales generated online, in China on so-called "Singles Day" on November 11, the Alibaba platform alone generated US$25 billion—ten times as much. In Germany, for example, it still sounds rather exotic to pay using a smartphone at the supermarket checkout; in China, it is a matter of course, even in very remote areas. At present, smartphone health apps are very popular among Chinese consumers; from 2016 to 2017 alone, the market grew by 75 percent.

MERCK IN CHINA

For Merck, the company which I lead, China plays a key role. It is our most important future growth market. Here we develop and produce medicines for the treatment of severe illnesses, technologies for the manufacture of medicines, materials that enable the production of smaller and faster microchips, and more. Merck is well positioned to benefit from many of the Chinese government programs described above. We want to help improve healthcare for Chinese patients and to foster the development of local high-tech industry. Today, we already have around 3,300 employees in China. We can learn a great deal from these diverse talents. Therefore, we want to integrate them much more strongly into our global organization.

Our company operates in numerous locations throughout China. In Beijing, we operate one of the four global hubs of our Biopharma business. In Nantong on the Yangtze Delta, we recently opened a new pharmaceutical production plant. Also in Nantong, we are currently setting up a new location for our Life Science business. In Shanghai, we are developing new OLED (organix light-emitting diode) technologies together with our clients. In the coming years, we want to expand our presence in China still further. As a science and technology company, we want to be a part of the Chinese innovation ecosystem. We are therefore, amongst other things, setting up an innovation hub in Guangzhou, where we work in close cooperation with local start-ups and founders. The same is true for Merck as for the market economy as a whole: our future is becoming a good deal more Chinese.

EUROPE SHOULD BE A STRONG PARTNER FOR CHINA

We should view China's development in a broader overall context. At present, we are seeing the emergence of a multi-polar world with a center of gravity in Asia. Europe is being marginalized, moved to the periphery. This multi-polarity is reflected in the parallel existence of different economic systems. Anglo-American and continental European-style market economies remain in existence, alongside rising, centrally planned economies such as that of China and others. Command economies like that of North Korea are fortunately an exception in today's world. The future of capitalism thus lies in a variety of manifestations. Alongside the long-dominant Western liberal model of market economics, with its decentralized decision-making structures, a politically administered variant is emerging in which the course set by the governing party is key.

We in Europe should view these different variants calmly. Their emergence is no reason for a system conflict. At the same time, however, we should be in no doubt about it: our own European economic order is about more than the efficient distribution of goods and services. Adam Smith himself was not only an economist, but also a moral philosopher. European-style market economics are firmly anchored in our fundamental values of democracy, freedom, and the rule of law. Efficiency and usefulness are necessary criteria for us, but they are never an end in and of themselves.

We should seek dialogue with China on the basis of our European values, and we should be a strong partner for the country, because we are connected by shared goals and interests, for example, a free, rules-based order for world trade in the framework of the World Trade Organization and, naturally, advances in science and technology that lastingly improve the lives of countless numbers of people.

Notes

1. https://wits.worldbank.org/CountryProfile/en/Country/CHN/ Year/2016/TradeFlow/Export (accessed November 16, 2018).

2. https://www.destatis.de/DE/ZahlenFakten/ GesamtwirtschaftUmwelt/Aussenhandel/Tabellen/ RangfolgeHandelspartner.pdf?__blob=publicationFile (accessed November 16, 2018).

3. http://appsso.eurostat.ec.europa.eu/nui/show.do?query=-BOOKMARK_DS-016890_QID_-27022A2D_UID_-3F17 1EB0&layout=FLOW,L,X,0;PARTNER,L,Y,0;PRODUC T,C,Z,0;PERIOD,L,Z,1;REPORTER,L,Z,2;INDICATOR S,C,Z,3;&zSelection=DS-016890PERIOD,201752;DS-01-6890PRODUCT,TOTAL;DS-016890REPORTER,EU28;DS-016890INDICATORS,VALUE_IN_

EUROS;&rankName1=INDICATORS_1_2_-
1_2&rankName2=PRODUCT_1_2_-1_2&rankNa
me3=PERIOD_1_0_0_0&rankName4=REPORTE
R_1_2_0_0&rankName5=FLOW_1_2_0_0&rank
Name6=PARTNER_1_2_0_1&sortR=ASC_0&rStp=&c-
Stp=&rDCh=&cDCh=&rDM=true&cDM=true&foot-
nes=false&empty=false&wai=false&time_mode=NONE&-
time_most_recent=false&lang=DE&cfo=%23%23%23%
2C%23%23%23.%23%23%23 (accessed November 16, 2018).

4. https://www.stiftung-mercator.de/media/downloads/4_
Partnergesellschaften/Merics/China_Flash.pdf (accessed
November 16, 2018).

5. https://www.foreignaffairs.com/articles/china/2018-08-13/
when-china-rules-web (accessed November 16, 2018).

6. https://www.foreignaffairs.com/articles/china/2018-08-13/
when-china-rules-web (accessed November 16, 2018).

7. https://data.worldbank.org/indicator/SP.DYN.LE00.
IN?locations=CN (accessed November 16, 2018).

8. https://www.forbes.com/sites/rebeccafannin/2018/04/06/
midas-list-2017-credits-china-vcs-and-unicorns-for-impact/
#69010c9c705e (accessed November 16, 2018).

9. https://home.kpmg.com/us/en/home/media/press-releas-
es/2018/01/2017-us-venture-capital-reaches-record-84-2b-
after-strong-q4.html (accessed November 16, 2018).

10. https://home.kpmg.com/sg/en/home/media/press-releases/
2018/01/kpmg-venture-pulse-q4-2017.html (accessed
November 16, 2018).

11. https://www.forbes.com/sites/ninaxiang/2018/10/05/chinas-
ai-industry-has-given-birth-to-14-unicorns-is-it-a-bubble-
waiting-to-pop/#671f93b646c3 (accessed November 16, 2018).

12. http://www.spiegel.de/wirtschaft/soziales/china-
bonitaetswaechter-warnen-vor-gigantischen-kreditrisiken-
a-1233540.html (accessed November 16, 2018).

CHAPTER 11

WHAT DOES CORRUPTION MEAN FOR THE MARKET ECONOMY? AN INTRODUCTION

CORINNE M. FLICK

Corruption on any significant scale is a dangerous problem for a state and its market economy. When corruption starts, states begin to fail. It undermines the structures of the state and especially the legal system. Corruption is something that strikes at the rule of law, posing a fundamental threat to society in general and to economic life in particular.

On the one hand, it destroys the foundation of the peaceful coexistence of citizens by creating increased inequality. In so doing, it generates a sense of frustration among those who lose out as a result of the advantages gained unfairly by the corrupt. On the other hand, corruption also takes away the economy's ability to function equitably. In the long run, corruption leads to a paralysis of economic life. It has a corrosive effect on the readiness of economic agents to invest and therefore reduces productivity. This has a negative effect on job opportunities and ultimately the rate of economic growth.

The word corruption comes from the Latin "*corrumpere*" which means, in its primary sense, "to break in pieces," hence to "spoil or destroy." The definition that the word "corruption" has come to acquire in the modern world is as a misuse of public power—or public trust—for private means. Not only can public officials commit crimes of corruption, but so too can CEOs, or managers of NGOs, who are also the custodians of a different form of public trust. Thus, corruption exists in all fields of human endeavor.

In traditional societies, transactions are based on relationships and favors. Modern market economies, in turn, function based on the rule of law where private favors are not allowed to interfere with economic interactions. Corruption threatens to send a modern society back into the habits of a traditional one.

The rule of law is one of the most precious qualities of modern, "free" societies. Without the rule of law, there is no order and nothing is predictable. Order is the place where the behavior of the world matches our expectations. It is the place where the often-invisible axioms you live by organize your experience and your actions so that what should happen does happen. This is a fundamental requirement for a well-ordered economic life. The rule of law is essential for the liberal organization of an economy. Corporations that want to take on responsibility need appropriately reliable framework conditions in which to work. These framework conditions can only be provided by the law.

Nevertheless, we should be aware that laws have an organic nature: they are changing, constantly developing and adapting. This is an important characteristic, as the functioning of law requires its social acceptance. If rules are too rigid or do not make sense, they will not be accepted, rather they will be circumvented.

This organic nature is reflected in a very strange phenomenon: small-scale corruption can be invigorating for economic life. It is a fine line between order and chaos, but exactly on the border between the two, life, as well as economic life, reveals itself as intense and fruitful. However, this should not be misunderstood. As soon as corruption exceeds the low level, it has a clearly negative correlation with economic growth.

Corruption is a severe form of law-breaking. A person who is open to corruption distances him- or herself from the rule of law. The following example demonstrates the global extent of corruption in the contemporary world: the International Monetary Fund (IMF) estimates the annual cost of bribery—which only accounts for part of all types of corruption—at 2 trillion USD, which is the equivalent of 2 percent of global GDP.[1]

Corruption exists in every country. It is a dangerous misconception to think that European states are exempted. Of course, the intensity in each country varies. If we look at the world map, we can roughly state that corruption in Southeast Asia and India is in a class of its own. In Europe, there is a remarkable upwards gradient of the corruption index between the Scandinavian countries and Switzerland, on the one hand, and the countries towards the East and the South, on the other hand. Interestingly, the gradient mirrors that of the average income in these economies. The lower the average household income, the higher the level of perceived corruption. In other words, as some commentators have observed, the more traditional the society is, the more the rule of law diminishes.

In that respect, Italy can serve as a suitable example. As is well known, there exist several organized crime syndicates; the Mafia in Italy is powerful. Taking advantage of the decade-long economic crisis in Italy, the country's organized crime syndicates have infiltrated the entire food chain: from production to distribution. Italy is the third biggest agricultural power in Europe. Illicit activities in this sector have become a highly lucrative income source for the criminal cartels. According to the Rome-based think tank, The Observatory of Crime in Agriculture and the Food Chain, their criminal activity in the food sector is more profitable than on the drug market, but much less dangerous. In a globalized industry, the Mafia's reach extends well beyond Italy's borders, reaching dinner tables around the world.[2]

Corruption as a type of law-breaking can be reduced, but as soon as we stop our efforts, it comes back again. Corruption knows no borders. Therefore, all of us have to work collectively in the fight against corruption. The larger the number of people who break the law, the more lacking in scruples the individual becomes. If everyone else evades taxes, for instance, we can all feel excused.

Lately, we have had to recognize that something as obvious as democracy requires continuous vigilance.

It is in no way an irreversible achievement. The same is true for the rule of law, which also needs ongoing attention and awareness to make sure that what has been achieved is maintained.

The judiciary system guarantees the functioning of the rule of law. Consequently, the kind of corruption that is most harmful to economic development is corruption of the judiciary or of the institutions, which are supposed to punish free-riders. Such corrupt practices ruin a country's reputation, as they erode trust as a general social framework.

In a conversation at the 2018 Convoco Forum between Alex Karp, the co-founder of Palantir Technologies, and Stefan Oschmann, the CEO of Merck, the latter said that the actual crisis of capitalism is that people do not trust the system any more.[3] As for national governments, for example, a Eurobarometer study from 2016[4] showed that there is a severe lack of trust: 64 percent of Europeans tend not to trust their governments.

There is a relationship between trust among citizens and the economic wellbeing of a state. It is proven that if there is a lack of interpersonal trust, this has a negative impact on productivity and GDP. The economy runs on the basis of trust. Interpersonal trust is the currency of the economy and an important resource. Generally, it can be stated that the stability of material things is more dependent on the integrity of the spirit than vice versa.[5]

ebay serves as a good example of this. The platform's economic model works only on trust. The seller tells the truth about the item they are offering, and the buyer pays the agreed price. When eBay started, it offered the possibility of insuring transactions for a 10 percent surcharge. These insurances soon became pointless as trust was and is the basis of this business model. This trust activated dead capital because goods, which were unsellable before, now became part of the economic cycle. As a consequence, economic growth was created.

This shows that trusting somebody, once one's eyes are open, is an act of courage—not naivety. If one shows one's hand, one will encounter openness and trust in the other person.[6] Trust in our economy and in our political system can be created through transparency, which is based upon the rule of law. Transparency, in turn, is a most important factor in the fight against corruption. Every effort to reduce this transparency, for instance, by campaigns against whistleblowers, is something that should set alarm bells ringing.

Speaking about the fight against corruption, we must recognize the important role played by institutions.

Institutions, in general, fulfil a key function in society. They limit the arbitrariness of individual action and represent two virtues which individuals often lack. First, they combine a long-term purpose with a notion of the common good. They can learn from the experiences of the many and incorporate them. Second, institutions cause human action to be considered and reflected upon and thus exercise an educational influence on their members. In our modern world, they are the best way of giving the long-term perspective a chance.[7]

Especially today, when problems concern the international community as a whole, institutions with global reach are vital. The IMF is one of these: 189 countries are part of it. It was established at the Bretton Woods Conference in 1944. Its primary purpose is to ensure the stability of the macroeconomic and international monetary system. Alongside other tasks and among its core targets are the reduction of poverty around the world and the fight against corruption.

The cooperation between civil society organizations, the state, the private sector, and international institutions is essential in the fight against corruption. The problem of corruption is global; it can infect a wide variety of economic areas and has the potential to infiltrate all sectors of society whether they are public or private. Corruption is a phenomenon of culture, and therefore the fight against it demands a change of culture. It is not enough to punish corruption. The aim must be a mutual understanding within society that corruption is harmful for the individual and for society as a whole.

Notes

1   International Monetary Fund, *Corruption: Costs and Mitigating Strategies*, IMF Staff Discussion Note no. 16/05, 2016, p. 5.

2   https://www.ft.com/content/73de228c-e098-11e8-8e70-5e22a430c1ad (accessed December 5, 2018).

3   http://www.convoco.co.uk/convoco-conversation-alexander-karp-and-stefan-oschmann (accessed December 5, 2018).

4   European Union, *Standard Eurobarometer 85 – Spring 2016: Public Opinion in the European Union, First Results* (European Union, 2015).

5   See Jordan Peterson, *The Secret to Combating Corruption in Society*, available on https://www.youtube.com/watch?v=aeDFcDcp6-U (accessed December 5, 2018).

6   Ibid.

7   Roger Scruton, "Being and Letting Be" in Corinne M. Flick (ed.), *To Do or Not To Do: Inaction as a Form of Action* (Munich: Convoco! Editions, 2015).

CHAPTER 12

ADDRESSING CORRUPTION—
WHY IT MATTERS

SEAN HAGAN

Over the past several years, there have been a number of high-profile corruption scandals that have—justifiably—generated considerable moral outrage. However, as important as this moral dimension may be, in this discussion I am going to focus on the broader economic, social, and political impact of corruption. More specifically, I will explain why this issue has become so relevant to the work of the International Monetary Fund (IMF), the institution that I worked for until very recently.

First, a word about the IMF. It was established at the end of World War II and the rationale for its creation is still very relevant today: economic nationalism is a threat to world peace and, in order to reduce this risk, countries need to make commitments regarding economic cooperation. What is extraordinary about the framework that was established over 70 years ago is that it not only involved the creation of treaty obligations regarding economic cooperation, but also the establishment of an independent institution—the IMF—that was charged with monitoring these obligations. Specifically, as a means of preventing financial crises, the IMF was given regulatory authority which involves making—and publishing—assessments regarding the quality of economic policies, including policies that support sustainable and inclusive economic growth. The IMF was also given financial powers to address crises when they do occur.

And it has become clear to the IMF that addressing systemic corruption is relevant for both of its roles in crisis prevention and crisis resolution. Later, I will explain why that is the case and what recommendations we have made to address this problem.

A word about definitions. While there are different definitions of corruption, the one that is most generally accepted—and which is relied upon by the Fund—is "the abuse of public office for private gain." There are a couple of points to be made with respect to this definition.

First, at a minimum, it includes those acts that almost all countries understand as criminal—in particular, bribery and embezzlement; i.e., the theft of funds. However, there are many who feel strongly that the concept should also include acts that, although not illegal, should be understood as being corrupt because they involve the public interest being compromised by private interests. This is particularly relevant in the political sphere, including in the area of campaign finance.

Second, the focus is on abuse of public office. The term does not cover abuses that take place exclusively within the private sector. However, the private sector is part of the problem and, therefore, must be part of the solution. For every bribe that is received by a public official, one is given by a private actor.

Finally, even though the term "corruption" may not be used to describe abuses, including fraud, that take place within the private sector, it does not mean that these practices are not harmful. As I will discuss, a key cause of the Great Financial Crises of 2008 was abuses within the financial services industry.

I would like to begin with abuses within the public sector. I should emphasize that all countries encounter corruption. My focus is those countries where corruption is systemic; i.e. where corrupt behavior is no longer the exception to the norm but has become the norm itself. In these circumstances, it has become clear that corruption undermines the ability of the state to support a market economy in a number of different respects.

A key state function is fiscal—the capacity of the state to raise money through taxation and to spend it on critical services. With respect to the taxation function, there are countries where tax evasion is widespread—particularly among the affluent, professional classes—and where the tax authorities are complicit in this practice. The failure of the wealthy to pay taxes completely delegitimizes the system: why should cab drivers pay their taxes when they know that doctors and lawyers do not?

What is the impact of this? As we have seen, widespread tax evasion can undermine fiscal sustainability and give rise to debt crisis. Indeed, this was one of the key causes of the crisis in Greece.

Perhaps even more problematic, however, is the effect that corruption can have on expenditure. First, there is the problem of waste, which occurs when there is corruption in the way the government purchases goods and services, relying on kickbacks and bribery in the procurement process. Second, and more fundamentally, corruption actually distorts spending decisions. Instead of investing in schools and public health, both of which are necessary to support inclusive growth, corrupt officials will prefer to build conference centers where kickbacks can be generated. Indeed, there is considerable evidence that, where corruption is systemic, it undermines the delivery of basic social services that the most vulnerable groups in society rely on. In this respect, systemic corruption not only undermines sustainable growth, it also exacerbates inequality.

A second state function that is distorted by corruption is the state's function as a regulator. While views may differ on the appropriate design of regulations, there is a general recognition that any functioning market economy needs to be supported by an effective regulatory framework. However, when corruption is systemic, this framework can be abused in a number of different ways.

For example, government officials will demand bribes in exchange for licenses, permits, and other types of approval that are typically needed for investment. This not only makes investment more expensive but, perhaps more importantly, it creates uncertainty that discourages investment in the first place. Imagine a foreign investor who is thinking of starting a factory in a country where corruption is systemic. When they are making the initial large capital investment, they need to consider that at every stage in the life of the project they may be requested to pay another bribe.

In that regard, there is a myth that businesses like corruption because it creates efficiency. There is indeed an expression that the only thing worse than a corrupt, inefficient government is a clean, inefficient government. In my view, this is indeed a myth. All of the business executives with whom I have spoken recognize that systemic corruption discourages business activity precisely because of the considerable uncertainty it creates.

A second way in which systemic corruption undermines the effective operation of a regulatory framework is through what is referred to as "state capture"—where powerful private interests bribe regulators to effectively suspend the application of regulatory requirements and to look the other way. In this scenario, the pressure for corruption does not come from the officials but from the private sector. This can have catastrophic consequences on the economy. Indeed, one of the causes of the Asian financial crisis was the excessive build-up of debt in the banking system. Regulators had effectively failed to exercise adequate supervisory oversight of these institutions because they were captured by powerful financial interests.

Of course, the problem of state capture also arises in other areas, including public safety. An example of this is the bribes paid by builders to building inspectors in Bangladesh that enabled them to build factories using substandard materials. One of these factories collapsed in 2013, killing over one thousand people.

Regulatory corruption is often referred to as petty corruption, so as to distinguish it from the theft of large amounts of money by political leaders, referred to as "grand corruption." But clearly, the impact of regulatory corruption is anything but petty.

More generally, as corruption becomes entrenched in all aspects of society it can have a debilitating psychological impact, particularly on young people, who become increasingly cynical. In a society where *who* you know is far more important than *what* you know, young people's interest in education naturally declines.

Indeed, at a certain point, systemic corruption can lead to civil disorder and armed conflict, as those that are excluded from the benefits of economic activity express their frustration at the elites who have distorted the system to their advantage. The Arab Spring was, in large part, motivated by a frustration with entrenched corruption.

How do we address this acute problem?

The natural reaction is to look for a magic bullet, which was certainly my impulse when I first started dealing with this issue over 20 years ago. The problem is that it is a disease that requires action on a number of fronts. As Einstein said, one should make solutions as simple as possible—but no simpler.

The key point is that corruption is not a crime of passion. It is a crime of calculation—so one needs to focus on changing the incentive structure.

Of course, a key incentive for someone who is contemplating a corrupt act is the fear of going to jail. For this reason, a credible threat of prosecution is essential. However, the difficulty with the establishment of the rule of law is that it requires more than just the adoption of legislation. It requires institutions that have the capacity to implement it. Where corruption is systemic, the police, the prosecution, and the courts are often corrupt, so enforcement is compromised. Indeed, based on my own experience, a law is as weak as the weakest institution that is charged with implementing it. The challenge is that institutional reform takes a considerable amount of time.

Not only is the establishment of a credible threat of prosecution difficult to achieve but focusing exclusively on criminalization can result in the abuse of an anti-corruption strategy for political purposes. Specifically, we have seen how aggressive prosecutions have been used by an incoming government against the previous one.

To ensure that reform is permanent—and not subject to the vagaries of the political process—there is a consensus that the incentive framework needed to combat corruption requires not just criminalization but also broader regulatory and administrative reforms. As will become clear, many of these reforms are not anti-corruption specific, they also have broader benefits.

Let me start with regulatory reform. In many cases, excessively complex and nontransparent regulatory systems exist for the sole purpose of giving government officials the opportunity to extract bribes. In India, more than a dozen permits are needed to open a small retail store. In many cases, therefore, deregulation provides benefits not only in terms of general economic activity but also as an anti-corruption tool. Technology can also be very beneficial: obtaining a license or permit online removes the human transaction that can often be the opportunity for a bribe. Of course, there are limits to the degree to which regulation can be eliminated or streamlined. As indicated—and as we have learned through previous financial crises—an independent and effective regulatory framework in critical areas is essential and, in these cases, corruption can undermine this effectiveness.

A second area of reform is increased transparency. Since corruption is normally a crime it is, by definition, a hidden activity. Accordingly, increased transparency can play an important role in preventing it. For example, the theft of significant resources by senior public officials—often referred to as "grand corruption"—can be effectively addressed by ensuring greater transparency with respect to how governments manage their own finances. Requiring all governmental transactions to be part of a published, central budget that is subject to independent audits can play an important role. Similarly, ensuring transparency and accountability with respect to state-owned enterprises—which is particularly important in countries that rely on natural resources—is essential.

Actions in this area will depend on the context. In Indonesia, where corruption in the judiciary was systemic, one of the most successful reforms was the requirement that the opinions giving the rationale for the decisions be published. This transparency made it much more difficult for judges to deviate from established legal principles.

A final—and critical—area is administrative reform. In the final analysis, the goal is to establish a professional civil service that is proud of its independence from private influence and public interference. Achieving this requires reforms in a number of areas. First, increases in salaries may need to be considered. In many countries, public sector salaries are so low that corruption is not an expression of greed but an act of survival. Second, it is important to put in place—and enforce—performance management systems which ensure that the hiring and firing of civil servants is conducted on the basis of merit. In Georgia, administrative reform played a central role in the elimination of corruption in the police: although a large number were dismissed, those that were retained received significant salary increases.

When contemplating corruption strategies, it is important to confront some generalizations—or perhaps myths—that are often made with respect to corruption.

The first myth is that systemic corruption is simply a reflection of the prevailing culture and that there are certain cultures that are simply more corrupt than others. In these cases, there is nothing to be done. Some elements of this statement are true: culture can be understood as reflecting the prevailing social norms in society and, as I indicated, corruption is systemic when it becomes the norm of behavior rather than the exception. But social norms change and there are a number of examples of societies that were—historically—extremely corrupt that have managed to address it effectively. For example, during the 19th century, the US civil service was notoriously corrupt. It was not until the early 20th century that it became meritocratic. Singapore was one of the most corrupt societies prior to its independence in the early 1960s. It is now one of the least corrupt.

What is the catalyst for change? In some cases, it is a crisis that leads to a social and political realignment. This was surely the case in Indonesia, where the financial crisis unleashed anti-corruption forces within society that helped topple President Suharto and put in place important anti-corruption institutions. Leadership can also play a critical role. In the case of Singapore, Prime Minister Lee Kuan Yew played a central role in designing and implementing an anti-corruption strategy—in part by setting an example through his own personal behavior.

Another myth about corruption is that democracy is always a powerful, anti-corruption force. In some cases, as in the case of Indonesia, this is true. The establishment of democracy did play a critical role there. In other countries, however, such as in India, the existence of democracy has not helped. It coexists with corruption in a very comfortable way. Indeed, in some countries, democracy will actually exacerbate corruption. There was a very specific reason why, during the 19th century, the US civil service was corrupt: political candidates would buy votes through promises of employment in the civil service. This type of practice still exists in a number of countries. In the US, there is no longer the problem of politicians buying voters. Nevertheless, there is a concern about voters effectively buying politicians through the electoral finance system. Some people would say that this is a form of legalized corruption, and whether one agrees with this characterization or not, the current system does raise issues about how the public interest can be compromised by private interest. At a minimum, it greatly enhances the power of the wealthy in the electoral process.

Until now, my remarks have focused on strategies directed at those countries where corruption is systemic. Over the years, however, there is a recognition that the problems in those countries are not entirely of their own making. Foreign investors from advanced—and often relatively corruption-free—countries are often part of the problem. As I indicated earlier, for every bribe that is accepted, one is given. Moreover, once the bribe has been given, the public officials do not generally invest the proceeds of these crimes in their own countries. Rather, they send them overseas to financial institutions in advanced economies that are willing to conceal them. Consequently, this is a global problem that requires a global solution: private actors in advanced economies are facilitating both the supply of bribes and the concealment of the proceeds of these bribes. The good news is that many advanced economies are recognizing their responsibility and have made commitments to limit the supply by criminalizing the offering of bribes to foreign officials. The OECD is the leader in this area. The Financial Action Task Force addresses the problem of concealment, putting in place rules that prevent the laundering of funds of "politically exposed persons."

The bad news is that enforcement of these frameworks is very uneven. For example, the USA is a leader in the enforcement of the OECD Convention. At the same time, when it comes to addressing concealment, it is less effective. When the Panama Papers scandal erupted several years ago, there was a lot of scrutiny of off-shore jurisdictions such as Panama that allow investors to set up shell companies where the true "beneficial" ownership is not revealed. However, as the Financial Action Task Force pointed out, one of the countries which continues to fall behind in requiring the disclosure of beneficial ownership is, in fact, the USA.

I would like to conclude with a discussion of practices that take place exclusively within the private sector. Why should we care about this? What is the public interest in regulating the way private actors behave towards each other? The financial crisis ten years ago provides some indication of the stakes involved. There is no doubt that this crisis was caused at least in part by unethical practices within the financial services industry. The problem there was not just one of fraud. Several years ago, I moderated a panel at the IMF where one of the participants was Justin Welby, the Archbishop of Canterbury. He pointed out that when someone is in a position of power—as many of these senior people in the financial services industry are—their acts of recklessness should be considered unethical, even in the absence of fraud, given the fact that the lives of so many people are directly affected by these acts.

What can be done about this? As with the public sector, one has to look at the incentive structure and, in that regard, a considerable amount of progress has been made. Since the financial crisis, there have been changes to the rules regarding minimum capital and reform of the supervisory frameworks. These modifications are all designed to reduce the ability of private institutions to take excessive risks. With respect to criminal enforcement to address fraudulent acts, the outcome has been mixed. Although there have been many high-profile penalties given to financial institutions for fraud, there have been very few prosecutions against individuals. By limiting enforcement to the imposition of financial penalties on companies, there is a risk that companies will just view these penalties as a cost of doing business.

In my view, however, there is an even larger issue here. If we place exclusive reliance on regulations and rules, we will simply invite circumvention. What we need is not a culture of compliance but a culture of values. Indeed, we need to have public officials and private actors who do the right thing even though no one is watching. How do we achieve this? Education can play a key role. Increasingly, institutions of higher education, including business schools, have made ethics a mandatory part of their curriculum. At the McDonough School of Business, Georgetown University, I have been involved in teaching a course that emphasizes how a regular practice of meditation can actually enhance the ability of the executives to see their work as an expression of service rather than just as an extension of their ego. As Mark Carney, the Governor of the Bank of England, has pointed out, business leaders need to avoid compartmentalizing their lives. Usually, they lead their personal lives—where they apply an ethical framework—separately from their business lives. They need to begin to see their professional work as a contribution to broader societal goals.

Adam Smith would have understood this. Although he is known as the father of laissez-faire economics and the invisible hand of the market, he also understood economics as being an extension of moral philosophy. He understood that the market would only work effectively if it is underpinned by trust. The famous baker that is featured in *The Wealth of Nations* would only be able to sell his bread to the butcher if the butcher trusted him. Indeed, the Latin for "credit" is *credere*—to trust. At the height of the financial crisis, when the interbank market was frozen and counterparties could not get liquidity, it was because the institutions could no longer trust the value of the financial products. The evaporation of trust creates not only financial instability, but also political instability. Traditional institutions both within the public and the private sectors are currently under attack because they are no longer trusted to act in the broader interest. The most powerful—the elites—are perceived to be only interested in looking after themselves. In order to preserve these institutions—and I do believe they need to be preserved, not destroyed—they need to be reformed. I would only like to emphasize that reform requires not just a change in the rules but also a shift in individual values.

CHAPTER 13

CAPITALISM AND THE TAX STATE

RUDOLF MELLINGHOFF

A. INTRODUCTION

Discussing the future of capitalism prompts the question of what conditions must be met for this economic form to function. The likely crucial factors are that goods and services are in private ownership, that there is legal certainty, and that the state ensures that it is possible to do business in a liberal, economic environment. At first sight, the political participation of citizens, and thus democracy, does not necessarily seem to be a condition for capitalism to function. However, the question arises as to whether private property and economic freedom can be guaranteed permanently in a state that does not conform to the principles of a democratic, constitutional state.

As a result, free economic activity as one of the basic requirements of capitalism can only develop if the state provides the conditions that allow an exchange of goods and services, if it ensures a financial market and a functioning banking system, and if legal rights are guaranteed by the state and, if possible, enforced through independent courts. Capitalism thus requires a market that not only has good infrastructure, but where other functional conditions are also guaranteed. An economic and social order in which a free-enterprise economy can develop on the basis of private property is made possible in the first place by internal and external security, a well-educated population, but also state monopoly on the use of force. There are, of course, no prescribed duties attached to the democratic, constitutional state. However, it is recognized that one of the mandatory duties of a state is to ensure internal and external security, to establish and defend the law, to guarantee minimum subsistence in line with human dignity, and to provide essential infrastructure.

In order to be able to guarantee the conditions necessary for capitalism to function, the state needs money. In a state where capitalism is to develop, the state leaves the production factors of labor and capital in private hands, and completely abandons any revenue-generating state enterprises. However, if the state does not generate revenue through its own economic activity, it is dependent on participation in the success of private business through state levies.

The tax state thus proves to be the ideal state form in which a free-market economy can develop. In a tax state, state and economy are separate. Unlike in socialist states with central administration, the state is not the owner of the means of production and, in principle, does not itself make production-related decisions. The socialization of the means of production is inconsistent with capitalism, and is the basis of communist and socialist conceptions of the state.

History shows how capitalism and the tax state developed simultaneously. In the second half of the 20th century, the advantages of capitalism and the concept of the tax state came to dominate. However, a freely democratic, social constitutional state must not only guarantee the requirements of doing business in a market economy, it also has a wide range of tasks associated with the welfare state, it redresses the

217

social disadvantages of capitalist systems, and it regulates private-sector business. This extent of the state's activity tends to rely on increasing government revenues. Therefore, the tax state also needs constitutional limits in order to ensure that business in the market economy can operate in the long term. This framework can be implemented easily under the conditions of conventional economic activity in a nation state. However, globalization and increasing digitalization are leading to fundamental changes and new challenges.

B. THE COMMON ORIGINS OF CAPITALISM AND THE TAX STATE

I. THE CONCEPT AND DEVELOPMENT OF CAPITALISM

Scholarly and political debates about capitalism begin in the second half of the 19th century and develop their full dynamic in the first half of the 20th century. In such debates, the concept of capitalism is not an unambiguous, clearly defined term, but an economic form that is discussed in its various characteristics and aspects. Towards the end of the 17th century, the term "capitalist" was associated with merchants, bankers, *rentiers*, and others who traded or brokered capital. In the course of the 19th century, an understanding of the concept emphasizing the difference between a capitalist and the workers came to predominate. In the late 19th and early 20th centuries, the difference between capitalism and socialism was developed from a critical and comparative perspective.

The definition of capitalism was coined decisively by Karl Marx, Max Weber, and Joseph A. Schumpeter. During the first half of the 20th century, other scholars specified and concretized the concept of capitalism and its various characteristics. But for all the differences in detail, we can still identify some defining features in the definition of capitalism:[1]

Capitalism requires private property rights and individual decision-making by market players. The resulting added value is assigned to the owners of the private property rights, and can consist of both profits and losses. Economic operators may be individuals, groups, companies, or other associations of economic operators.

Another key feature of capitalism is the realization of profits in the market. In doing so, the various actors participate through competition and cooperation, using supply and demand, and the purchase and sale of goods and services. This market participation requires a functioning monetary economy and acquires its particular dynamics through the division of labor.

The very word "capitalism" implies that capital is fundamental to this way of doing business. A functioning capital market, which also enables investment and reinvestment through the raising and granting of loans, is also seen as an essential feature of capitalism. This enables business to be transacted over the longer term, the creation of savings, and investment in future returns. At the same time, one element of capitalism is the uncertainty and risk that go with investment decisions.

Further hallmarks of capitalism are acquisitiveness and maximizing profits through the rational organization of labor and market dominance. This requires the pre-eminence of free and dynamic entrepreneurship and often leads to the creation of large entrepreneurial companies. However, it is debatable whether the existence of a company or a venture is a defining characteristic of capitalism. Notwithstanding, capitalism favors companies that are organized in a capitalistic way and that differentiate between dependent employees without capital and production assets on the one hand and entrepreneurs on the other.

The question of when capitalism came into being is answered in different ways by scholars. Trade and commerce, the pursuit of profit, and the willingness to take economic risks have always existed. The beginnings of capitalistic trade can thus be observed early on the activities of merchants. Long-distance trade is often cited as evidence for the development of the early manifestations of capitalism: examples can be seen in the Roman Empire, China's Han dynasty (206 BCE–220 CE), and the Arab empires of the Umayyads and Abbasids of the late 7th to mid-13th centuries. Today, we are still familiar with the major trade routes such as the Silk Road and trade associations such as the Hanseatic League.

The Enlightenment brought the first engagement with the theoretical requirements of a type of economy that served prosperity and focused on the freedom of the individual. Alongside Montesquieu, Hobbes, Locke, and Spinoza, Adam Smith deserves special mention. In his fundamental work, *An Inquiry Into the Nature and Causes of the Wealth of Nations*, he described the essential elements of capitalist business such as the division of labor, capital accumulation, supply and demand, trade and the market as prerequisites of a rational and prosperous economic system. It is not surprising that Adam Smith's key reflections and ideas are still used and quoted by economists and social scientists today.

But it was only over the course of 19th-century industrialization that capitalism developed into the economic form, which became the subsequent topic of theoretical and scientific research. With the invention of mechanical production methods and efficient processes for the exploitation of coal, iron, and steel, the mass production of economic assets could develop, significantly changing economic and social conditions, working conditions, and living conditions. Only with the Industrial Revolution do we see capitalism beginning to be the subject of scientific and theoretical debate in the late 19th and early 20th century. During industrialization, large corporations and business combinations emerged that turned wage labor into a mass phenomenon. At the same time, technological and organizational innovations developed at an unprecedented speed. This resulted in the next form of capitalist economy, which in the course of the 20th century expanded in various versions, increased prosperity in many countries, and at the beginning of the 21st century proved to be a superior economic form by comparison with socialist states.

II. THE CONCEPT AND DEVELOPMENT OF THE TAX STATE

Just as old as the economic activity of individuals, especially merchants, is taxation. From early antiquity onwards, there are reports of customs duties, tithes, and tributes. The first evidence of levies at an international level appears in the third millennium BCE in Egypt. But like capitalism, taxation in the modern sense did not develop until the 19th century; and only the 20th century saw the development of the tax state as we know it.

Until well into the 19th century, states covered their expenditures primarily using revenues from their demesne lands, the earliest and at that time most productive sources of public revenue. The state demesne lands were properties belonging to the state, and so the revenue first and foremost consisted of work-related income. In the 18th century, it was argued that a state should be able to manage without taxes, but soon people began to consider the question of taxation. During the French Revolution, the principles of universality and fairness in taxation were developed. England was the first to introduce a graduated income tax at the end of the 18th century. In the course of the 19th century, and at the same time as the beginning of industrialization, states universally started raising taxes in the modern sense. Gradually, all the individual German states introduced taxes to meet their financial needs. Over time, taxation replaced government revenue from demesne lands as the state's primary source of income.

It is more than an astonishing parallelism that, in the same work where he first discussed a new economic order and a capitalist welfare state, at the same time Adam Smith laid down the fundamental principles of taxation. He demanded:

1. "The subjects of every state ought to contribute towards the support of the government, as nearly as possible, in proportion to their respective abilities, that is, in proportion to the revenue which they respectively enjoy under the protection of the state."

2. "The tax that each individual has to pay must be certain and not arbitrary. The time of payment, the manner of payment, the quantity to be paid ought all to be clear and plain to the contributor, and to every other person."

3. "Every tax should be levied at the time or in the manner in which it is most convenient for the contributor to pay it."

4. "Every tax should be so contrived as both to take out and to keep out of the pockets of the people as little as possible over and above what it brings into the public treasury of the state."[2]

At the end of the 19th century, Lorenz von Stein could state that tax "surpasses all other state revenues so much that they seem almost unimportant by comparison."[3] Revenues from duties, demesne lands, and other minor charges were no longer enough to finance state activity. The general tax liability became the only reliable state revenue. It is not surprising, therefore, that towards the end of the 19th century, economists developed the essential, theoretical foundations of taxation that still apply today.

Although, by the end of the 19th century, the main burden of government revenue was already the result of taxes, their amount was extraordinarily low by today's standards.

Those economists who developed and described the theoretical foundations of capitalism also devoted themselves to the topic of taxation. While the universality and fairness of taxation was something both constitutional lawyers and economists agreed upon, the debate was also partly about the impact of taxation on the economy. Lorenz von Stein justified taxation with the fact that the individual could not achieve economic returns without the support of the community constituted by the state, adding that through taxes the individual gave back to the community only part of the economic growth they had gained as a result. This principle of the justification of taxation linked Stein with the requirement to limit the power of taxation; in particular, taxes should not affect capital. The tax state, Stein claimed, depended on the economy and would be a threat to its existence if it attacked its very substance.

The economist Joseph A. Schumpeter was also concerned about the efficiency and growth of the economy, as the explosion of expenditure post-World War I could lead to higher taxation and thus to an excessive burden on the economy. Schumpeter warned that higher taxation would require an "army of bureaucrats to enforce tax laws, tax inquisition would become more and more intrusive, and tax chicanery more and more unbearable." Thus, he said, the tax state, which is rooted in the autonomy of the private economy and private life, would lose its meaning.[4]

The modern, democratic, constitutional state covers its financial needs mainly through taxes, but the tax state is not just a description of public finance through taxation. Rather, the idea and concept of the tax state are sustained by the fact that the state is not itself commercially active, but participates in the success of private business activity through taxation. An essential feature of the tax state is that state and economy are separate. Ideally, the state creates the economy's actual and legal framework and limits, but does not itself participate in the economy as an agent. Within the given framework, the economy should be able to develop freely and organize on its own behalf. This guarantees private property and fundamentally free enterprise as two basic prerequisites of capitalism.

Paul Kirchhof clearly summarizes the idea of the tax state and a financing of the state that is based on freedom when he writes:

> The constitutional state guarantees occupational freedom and the freedom to own property, leaving the production factors of labor and capital in private hands and structurally dispensing with state-owned enterprises that could create revenue for the state. Labor and economic assets are generally used privately by persons entitled to freedom of choice; the free state is to this extent excluded from the management of these sources of income. The state is relegated to participating in the success of private business through taxes. Tax income depends on the result of private services; the public and private realms are united by a common interest in a prospering economy.[5]

Of course, the tax state is not a prerequisite for a capitalist economy. It may also be conceivable that states can be financed less by taxes and more by capital charges, such as fees and contributions. However, the fact that the Western capitalist economic model has essentially prevailed in those countries that have signed up to the idea of the tax state shows just how successful this interaction between the market economy and the tax state is. Irrespective of this, the principle of the tax state is most closely related to the idea of a liberal, democratic, constitutional state, in contrast to a state which is primarily financed by other revenues, such as capital charges that are imposed on specific beneficiaries according to the principle of equivalence. The tax state relies on the democratic, parliamentary concept of the constitutional state. The fundamental separation of revenue and expenditure at the level of the state budget as well as the fundamental absence of fiscal ringfencing not only enables the equitable participation of citizens in public financing, but also broadens the state's ability to act in general.

C. SOCIAL MARKET ECONOMICS AND THE LIMITS OF THE TAX BURDEN

In the period between the development of the notion of the tax state in the second half of the 19th century and its realization in the second half of the 20th century, conditions changed many times. The capitalism of the Industrial Revolution evolved into a concept of social market economy. In this way, the advantages of the free market economy were to be reconciled with the principle of the welfare state. The expansion of the welfare state and the continuous expansion of state activity lead inevitably to growing financial needs. The history of the tax state is characterized by a steady increase in state tasks, an expansion in government revenue, and the deepening of taxation. However, the limitation of or even reduction in the tax burden is really the result of international tax competition.

A *de facto* limitation of the tax burden on companies can result from tax competition between competing states. Increasing globalization and internationalization, the changing nature of business activity, and the associated mobility have meant that the tax burden plays an increasingly important role in the decisions companies make about location. By lowering corporation taxes, creating targeted tax exemptions for a certain period of time, tax incentives for certain types of income and activities, or low-key tax compliance, governments seek to attract international investors and businesses. Since the 1980s, this has meant that major industrialized countries have significantly reduced their corporation tax rates up until the beginning of this millennium. Whether and to what extent the reduction in corporation tax rates has led to an actual reduction in the tax burden on companies is debatable, since tax-rate reductions are usually accompanied by a broadening of the tax base through the reduction of benefits, restrictions on offsetting options and loss relief, a tightening-up of the way provisions are created, or other tax-increasing measures.

All in all, even in a tax state whose concept is based on participation in the success of the private sector, the steady expansion of state activity requires a limitation of the tax burden in order to give businesses and individuals the opportunity to enjoy their entrepreneurial freedom and thus create prosperity. On the one hand, such limits may arise from the constitution of a state. On the other hand, international tax competition means that states gain this freedom through the restrained taxation of companies and individuals.

D. THE CHALLENGES OF GLOBALIZATION AND DIGITALIZATION

This brief overview of the history and evolution of capitalism and the tax state shows that both have their roots in the early 19th century, both developed in the second half of the 19th century, and both established their essential features at the beginning of the 20th century. In the second half of the 20th century, capitalism developed into a social market economy that ensured entrepreneurial freedom, at the same time consolidating and expanding the welfare state, and proving superior to socialist economic models. The tax state as a model of freedom-oriented public finance has been a crucial accompaniment to this development. Growing prosperity and the development of an enhanced welfare state, however, also led to growing government spending and a steady increase in tax revenues.

Of course, capitalism in its purest form has been exposed to criticism that is in part justified. However, it has proved to be the superior economic system, especially in the form of the social market economy. Free enterprise is and remains the pillar of a liberal, democratic, constitutional state. In addition to numerous critical voices, there are also those who emphasize the positive aspects of capitalism. A good example of this is the eminent social historian and former president of the Social Science Research Center Berlin (WZB) Jürgen Kocka, who writes in his book, *Capitalism: A Short History*:

> Anyone who takes a serious look at the history of capitalism and, moreover, knows something about life in centuries past that were either not capitalist or barely so, cannot but be impressed by the immense progress that has taken place in large parts of the world (although not in all!). There has been progress above all for the many people who are not members of a well-situated upper class, progress with respect to material living conditions and overcoming poverty, gains in life span and health, opportunities for choice, and freedom. It was progress of which one may say, in retrospect, that it would presumably not have happened without capitalism's characteristic way of constantly stirring things up, pressing them forward, and reshaping them. And whoever would rather invoke different explanatory factors, like the growth of knowledge, technological change, or industrialization, as the real motors of progress should recall that, so far, any industrialization successful over the long run has everywhere presupposed capitalism. Capitalism's principles, moreover, have also done much to disseminate knowledge, which can be seen from the history of the media, starting with the printing of books, through the political press, to today's Internet. Thus far, all alternatives to capitalism have proven inferior, both with respect to the creation of prosperity and the facilitation of freedom.[6]

Today, capitalist economic models and public finances based on taxation are faced with completely new challenges created by globalization and digitalization.

The financial and economic crisis and the Euro crises of the past decade have shown that even a capitalist economic system is vulnerable. The international networking of financial markets and the globalized economy were suddenly faced with totally new challenges. It became clear that the effects of the global financial crisis were not limited to the financial markets, but also had consequences for the real economy. Although the economies in many countries have now recovered, the danger of another crisis in the capitalist economic system cannot be ruled out.

Since the beginning of the 21st century, digitalization has affected almost all areas of life. In a short period of time, modern information technology has transformed the economic and working environment, influencing social behavior, communication, and the political process, and penetrating into the individual's private world. Technological progress, increasing automation, and artificial intelligence raise the question of how capitalism and the social market economy are coping with these challenges.

The changes brought about by digitalization and globalization not only have an impact on entrepreneurship, but also create new challenges for the tax state. In a globalized world, capital income and intangible assets in particular are easy to relocate, so the associated tax avoidance strategies have an impact on tax revenue in high-tax countries. In an internationally networked economy, companies are in principle free to mitigate taxation through legal fiscal instruments. In recent years, this has led to intensive cooperation between tax authorities at an international level, in order to reduce the impact on national budgets.

Digitalization, in particular, poses new challenges for the tax state. Traditional taxation is based on companies that have a physical presence in a country, and whose respective source of income is visible and thus relatively easy to determine. Digitalization has created the need to tax easily transferable and hard-to-quantify intangible assets, data, and services that are mobile and often lack the physical presence of a business. This means that the current tax arrangements are being applied to cross-border trade and the provision of services without a physical presence. Current tax law is based on the traditional trade in goods and services, paid for using traditional currencies. Digitalization turns data into the new currency, without tax law being adjusted to take account of this change.

Both companies and states are facing new and formidable tasks that can only be tackled jointly. At the same time, traditional models of economic activity and public finance will have to change and adapt. However, the starting point must still be liberal, democratic principles that guarantee human dignity, safeguard private property, and at the same time realize the social, constitutional state.

Notes

1. On this conceptual definition, see the extensive discussion in Jürgen Kocka, *Capitalism: A Short History*, trans. Jeremiah Riemer (Princeton NJ: Princeton University Press, 2017), p. 16 ff.

2. By this, he meant that tax collection should incur as little money and expense as possible.

3. Lorenz von Stein, *Lehrbuch der Finanzwissenschaft*, 1885 f., Th. II, pp. 346 f.

4. Quoted in Hans-Peter Ullmann, *Der deutsche Steuerstaat* (Munich: C.H. Beck, 2005), p. 7 f.

5. Paul Kirchhof, "Die Steuern" in Josef Isensee and Paul Kirchhof, *Handbuch des Staatsrechts der Bundesrepublik Deutschland* (Heidelberg: C.F. Müller, 2003–2015) 3rd edn., vol. V, § 118, p. 960.

6. Kocka, *Capitalism*, p. 164.

CHAPTER 14

DIGITAL CAPITALISM AND ITS FISCAL CONSEQUENCES

WOLFGANG SCHÖN

Capitalism, as we know it, is restricted in three ways:

- Capital requires labor: Karl Marx knew that the capitalist's means of production would be worthless without the help of the worker as producer. Only the combination of labor and finance capital creates the goods that can succeed in the market.

- Finance capital must be transformed into real capital. The capitalist acquires land, builds factories, sets up machinery, and buys raw materials.

At the same time, this leads to the localization of capital: the investment is "sunk" in a specific place.

- The return on capital is not unlimited. Increased production requires increased employment of labor and increased capital investment. Although economies of scale and synergies may increase productivity, nevertheless there are natural limits to output.

Digital capitalism has liberated itself from all three of these constraints:

- Capital needs less labor than before. It takes very few engineers to supervise robot-controlled factories. Research and development require highly specialized experts, not an army of assembly-line workers. In the future, "artificial intelligence" may also make intellectual work superfluous to the same extent that robotics has for the most part replaced manual labor.

- Finance capital is increasingly being transformed into intangible assets. The drivers of value are not factories but algorithms, not machines but patents, not sales outlets but online presences and network effects. This leads to the delocalization of capital: as a company's most valuable resources, intangible assets can be allocated in any way as required.

- Returns on capital have no natural limits. A successful, intangible product can be manufactured and marketed as often as required, without significant extra costs. No additional workers have to be hired and hardly any additional machines have to be set up to stream a successful YouTube video millions of times, or to market the latest app at a global level.

The consequences are clear: the labor factor's share in economic success in terms of gross national product is falling. The owners of real capital are losing market power and are being remunerated at marginal prices. The owners of proprietary intangible assets or unique networks are creating monopolies and can make huge profits. These profits are accumulated where the intangible assets are located, i.e. no longer at fixed production locations or in the marketplace. We are witnessing a concentration of profits in the hands of the few and, at the same time, those profits becoming more mobile across national borders.

What does this mean for the fiscal state and its ability to provide public goods and organize redistribution in the social interest? In the first place, the answer lies in the laws of tax competition: the tax burden falls on immobile production factors—and in the era of digital capitalism these are precisely the production factors whose share in the gross national product is falling, namely real capital and labor. Intangible capital is elusive—and over recent years it has increasingly taken refuge in tax havens. On the one hand, this creates pressure on the overall tax revenue, but it also makes it increasingly difficult to use this tax revenue for redistribution purposes. After all, it is the very owners of these mobile assets who ought to make sacrifices under the principle of taxation according to ability to pay.

How can tax systems protect themselves against this erosion of their political power? The G20 and the OECD have tried to provide an initial response with their Action Plan to combat "Base Erosion and Profit Shifting" (BEPS), which was drafted between 2013 and 2015 and has since been implemented by over 100 countries through international agreements, European directives, or national legislation. The basic idea of the BEPS Action Plan is simple: the fiscal consequences of moving intangible assets into tax havens should be neutralized, and profits taxed where they are actually generated. The location of finance capital or intangible capital should not be the decisive factor in allocating taxing rights, but rather the location where the value is created, whether through research and development, through sales and marketing, or through corporate management functions.

In effect, this idea can be of great help in combatting tax evasion in tax havens—but in the end it is not decisive, as no one is preventing companies from increasing their staff numbers in tax havens and thus allocating profits tax-effectively to pay for their operations. Ultimately, tax competition also affects the "real economy": research and development departments can be relocated to low-tax countries and preferential regimes exploited. In the case of digital products, in particular, whose manufacturing and distribution no longer require close proximity to the customer, competition between countries to become the residence of value-creating business units will intensify. In this case, such competition no longer concerns just the relocation of "profits on paper" but of entire production sites—along with personnel and investments.

One way of stabilizing tax revenues, even in times when the business world is undergoing digitalization, is to shift fiscal rights of access to "market states," i.e.

the countries where the consumers of the products are based. The logic of tax competition supports this policy, because consumers are as immobile as employees. In recent decades, the global triumph of sales taxation (in the form of value-added tax) has provided the surest indication of the attractiveness of this form of taxation. For a long time now, rates of sales tax have been rising everywhere because the consumer cannot avoid it (apart from the few instances of consumer tourism). The reach of sales taxation, with all its practical implementation problems, is also being extended to transnational digital services. And even for seemingly free services, such as the use of Internet search engines or participation in social networks, it would be advisable to impose a sales tax burden on the major Internet service providers, because in actual fact these services are also paid for (the customer may not pay with money but by providing personal data, which in turn enables targeted promotions).

Certainly, such an extension of sales tax liability would be superior to a special tax as currently recommended by the European Commission for digital services in the European Union and already implemented by some States. A special tax on digital products would act as a punitive tax in the absence of sufficient economic or social policy reasons, as is the case with taxes on tobacco, alcohol, or fuel. Equally, any attempt to ring-fence the digital economy from the rest of the economy in terms of the chargeable event seems hopeless. The real economy is here to stay in the "Internet of Things," where power plants and motor vehicles alike collect and send data, benefit from algorithms, and create networks. And finally, such special taxes have also encountered political resistance, as has been the European Union's painful experience over the past ten years, in the example of the financial transactions tax, which is demanded by many but actually wanted by no one.

However, the EU-supported demand to raise taxes on digital services based on user location is coinciding with a more far-reaching trend: not only are customer states being granted access to the sales-tax revenue relating to the provision of services, but taxation that includes traditional taxes on profits (income taxes, corporation taxes) is also being relocated to the customer state. For example, in the run-up to the most recent US tax reform, there was intense debate about the proposal to levy corporation tax on international companies in the destination country. Traditional industrialized nations such as the Federal Republic of Germany are fearful of this, because such a shift in taxation rights would of course reduce the tax revenue in traditional export countries. Emerging and developing countries, in particular, which see themselves more in the role of customer states, have recognized this and are calling for a fundamental upgrading of the "markets" in the international distribution of the tax base. So it is no surprise that thus far in the international bodies of the G20 and the OECD no consensus has been found as to the right answer to the tax challenges posed by the digital economy.

What are the provisional findings? In the age of digital capitalism, we can expect that traditional taxes on profits will decline, against the background of the acceleration of international tax competition described above. However, the burden on consumers will increase. Taxes on private consumption are, however, ill-suited to reducing inequality in society. Is there a solution?

Progressive thinkers such as Thomas Piketty have used the argument of growing inequality to argue in favor of a global wealth tax that demands a substantial contribution from the "rich," wherever they are located. Others talk about stepping up income tax or inheritance tax. However, such demands can only be enforced if the politicians can deal successfully with tax competition. And this competition exists not only for companies, but also for high net-worth individuals and world-class professionals, such as artists and athletes. The past few years have shown that not only tax havens, but also traditional industrialized countries are increasingly offering major tax benefits to mobile "natural persons," if they change their residence. Today, Italy, Portugal, and even Sweden are offering a mobile elite fiscal framework that in previous years could only be exploited in Switzerland or England at most. And many countries have—as has the Federal Republic of Germany—abolished or greatly reduced the burden of net wealth taxes or inheritance taxes, at least for business owners. Under these conditions, it is not easy for individual states to enact socially motivated tax redistribution easily. An issue for future tax policy is whether, in an era of falling corporation tax, this race to the bottom can actually be stopped by countries agreeing on a common minimum level, at least with regard to the taxation of natural persons. At the moment, we are a long way from achieving that.

CHAPTER 15

PLATFORM CAPITALISM: THE NEXT STAGE OF ECONOMIC EVOLUTION

GISBERT RÜHL

Seven of the world's ten biggest companies are platform companies: Apple, Google, Microsoft, Amazon,
and Facebook from the US, alongside Alibaba and
Tencent from China. Together, these companies are
worth more than three and a half trillion euros.[1] This
is more than the Federal Republic of Germany's gross
domestic product in 2017.[2] The economic success
of platform companies cannot be compared with
conventional companies. But why are these companies
so extremely successful? A simple answer is that platforms make life easier; that's why people love them.

They give customers what they expect today—simple, customer-oriented solutions. As a result, more and more industries are organizing themselves using platforms, even in the manufacturing industries.

FROM GUILDS TO PLATFORM CAPITALISM

Ever since trade in commodities and something resembling coordinated economic processes or economic systems have existed, they have undergone transformations. While members of similar professional groups simply co-existed until the late Middle Ages, the first guilds finally emerged shortly before the turn of the first millennium. Guilds organized the key issues regarding individual professions in villages or towns and established the fundamental standards. This ensured the quality of the services provided, as good practices, for example, were mandatory. However, this also suppressed innovation.

Over the centuries, ownership of the means of production transferred increasingly into private hands. Where personal gains were to be made, an increasingly profit-oriented form of production arose, often at the expense of people and the natural world. More and more markets were opened up. Supply was extended increasingly across village, city, and national borders, until ultimately the boundaries for products, production, and the distribution of services and physical commodities were completely removed by companies that were operating at a global level.

Now, in the age of the fourth industrial revolution, with all its attendant opportunities, a major upheaval in the entire economic system is on the agenda. Today, we can already see that in more and more industries, digital platforms are intervening between buyers and sellers of products and services, and thus between established companies and their customers. As a result, a powerful feeling of alienation is emerging between service providers and service users—that is, between companies and customers. Power is also shifting because data often no longer reaches the companies, but remains with the platform operator.

Now a public issue, platform capitalism describes a new digital economic system, namely an enhanced form of capitalism. Capitalism is essentially defined as "private ownership of the means of production." In the age of platform capitalism, this relationship is in part dissolved: private ownership of information becomes the constituent principle of platform capitalism. In this economic system, digital platforms act as middlemen ("intermediaries"), bringing together supply and demand in the market, regardless of whether it is a physical product, a service, or a combination of both. Initially, this sounds straightforward and unspectacular. However, this development undermines the mechanisms of the market economy.

CHARACTERISTICS OF DIGITAL PLATFORMS AND THEIR FORMS

Platforms can undermine these mechanisms because they possess unique features:[3]

- They have access to almost *all the data concerning buyers and sellers*

- They have minimal capital commitment, as they generally *do not have large amounts of their own assets*

- They are thus *easily scalable without much capital expenditure*

- They allow *transaction costs to approach zero*

- They can *operate internationally without major expense*

- They can *create powerful network effects.*

These unique features apply to any type of platform, regardless of whether they are horizontal platforms with standard, cross-sectoral products or services, or vertical platforms with a variety of specialized products or services for specific customer groups or industries.

Probably the most straightforward type of platform is the *advertising platform*.[4] In this area today, the leading platform operators in the Western world include Google and Facebook. Both provide a virtually free service (search engine and social network), and monetize the information they have about their users by selling advertising space to advertisers. Initially, that sounds and is relatively straightforward.

Another rapid growth sector in recent years has been cloud platforms, as companies increasingly shift their business activities to the cloud.[5] *Cloud platforms*, such as Amazon Web Services (AWS), provide computing power or virtually unlimited storage capacity at the touch of a button. In this way, companies can buy flexibility and reduce the amount of capital they have tied up in the company's infrastructure. And the cloud provider gains access to another source of data.

Some of these platforms have also expanded to become product platforms by means of virtual products or services such as streaming (Netflix, Spotify, and YouTube). *Product platforms* dramatically reduce the cost of the product, so their marginal costs are almost zero.[6] Of course, this type of platform can also be applied to physical products such as cars. In some major cities, DriveNow offers vehicles for short-term rental, billed by the minute. In this case, however, the hardware provided belongs to the platform operator.

Lean platforms go one step further.[7] The best-known platforms of this kind are probably Uber or Airbnb. They do not own any rentable assets of their own. They just put the customer in touch with the owner of an asset or with people who have particular skills, and they take a transaction fee for providing this mediation process, payment processing, etc.

As we have already seen, these business models are increasingly being adopted in industry. For example, various *industrial platforms* offer infrastructure, software, or entire platform solutions (infrastructure plus analysis).[8] As the Industrial Internet of Things (IIoT) advances, the power and the market for industrial platforms that analyze data and/or provide infrastructure is growing.

EVERYTHING HAS ITS UPS AND DOWNS—FOR USERS AND SUPPLIERS

At user level, platforms provide many benefits, but there are also some disadvantages.

For the end consumer, alongside various advantages, participation in platforms generally increases the consumer surplus in the short term. Increased price transparency reduces the prices of the commodities on offer. At the same time, products and services can usually be rated. Accordingly, the quality of the service provided or of the product also becomes more transparent. If users want to swap their product for an equivalent one, the costs of switching fall to almost zero. Access to complementary products or substitutes also improves. We are all familiar with Amazon's simple but effective message "Customers also bought," which helps you select a suitable case for a cell phone, for example. Or in the industrial equipment sector, we might imagine a message such as "Similar machines with this malfunction break down less using this oil." The offers and improvements provided via network effects significantly increase a platform's usefulness.

A similar picture is emerging for the suppliers, for whom participation in several platforms or one large one opens up new digital distribution channels, and previously hard-to-reach target groups become accessible. Advertisements for their own products can also be directed in a targeted way towards premium advertising spaces. In combination with good customer service, companies operating in the market have access to customers from all over the world.

But with all these upsides, there are also downsides. In order to be able to offer bespoke services to customers, the platform operators must know as much as possible about them. This is why they collect as much data as possible that is, above all, as structured as possible. In 2015, for example, Stanford University found out that through just 70 "Likes," Facebook can predict the user's behavior better than the person's own friends—and over 300 "Likes" can make predictions that are even better than the person's own spouse.[9]

As we have already seen, this layer between suppliers and customers means that suppliers are losing direct contact with their customers. As in the case of the platform user, the supplier's dependence on the platform increases as the company gets bigger. In addition, competitive pressure increases due to the transparency in the platform itself. If we believe in market-based mechanisms, that is not such a bad thing, as competition encourages innovation. In the end, the better product will prevail.

PLATFORM OPERATORS ARE WINNING—
COMPETITION IS BECOMING ALGORITHMIC

Unfortunately, this is not always the case. Without effective regulation, the main beneficiary of a dominant platform will always be the operator, who has the opportunity of establishing rules to which both suppliers and users are subjected. Theoretically, the operator even has the opportunity of excluding suppliers and users—thereby significantly influencing competition. Once operators reach a certain, critical size, this feature becomes crucial. Imagine, for instance, that Google excludes one particular B2C company from advertising on GoogleAds or appearing in search-engine results. Suddenly, this creates major obstacles that affect whether the supplier can operate in the market at all.

The purchasing behavior of individual customers— and the resulting data—means that platforms are increasingly able to predict future purchasing behavior. Today, we constantly receive reminders that a particular product might have to be replaced or is almost running out, or which products might interest us. In future, however, we might also imagine that products will be replenished directly. In the industrial sector in particular, this approach would be conceivable in order to prevent "just-in-sequence" supply chains from collapsing as a result of human error. In such a case, however, it would be algorithms that increasingly decide which supplier is chosen. Competition would then take place on the platform via the algorithm.

NATURAL MONOPOLISTIC TENDENCIES REQUIRE EFFECTIVE REGULATION

The more attractive the offers, the more users will flock to the platform. The more users flock to the platform, the more suppliers who want to sell their products or services will use it. It is natural that monopolistic tendencies result from the major benefits of network effects. Once established, its size and market power prevent the existing platform from challenging these tendencies in open competition.

In order to allow alternatives to these monopoly platforms to emerge, the competition authorities would have to intervene as a corrective. However, effective regulation seems to be difficult in the case of supranational and sometimes highly diversified companies, and so requires an internationally coordinated approach. The aim must be to ensure competition and include the platforms within the same legal framework that applies to other companies in the sector. However, this often fails because the laws were not developed for this type of business. The platforms' continual launch of new products and services means that legislation is constantly under threat of playing catch-up with developments.

PLATFORMS ARE THE FUTURE—BUT IT DEPENDS ON THE CORRECT FORM

There are alternative models to monopolistic platforms. Two key approaches are cooperative and public platforms. Cooperative platforms do not belong to one single company, but are owned by several companies or their respective users. Investors provide the platform with capital to promote their strategic interests. The financial benefit comes not only from investment in the platform, but also from increased revenues generated in the normal course of business.

Accordingly, decisions are not made by individual persons, but collectively. Of course, this democratization of decision-making can greatly slow down the decision-making process. At the same time, the beneficiaries of the platform are an integral part of the platform itself, and this reduces the risk of possible exploitative tendencies among monopolistic platforms. In addition, access to data about the company is protected, as the participating companies can access all platform-generated data that would otherwise only be accessible to the platform operator. As a result, the alienation between companies and customers we mentioned earlier is avoided.

Conversely, however, this platform model is less attractive to purely financial investors than are platforms with monopolistic tendencies, for example. Ultimately, monopolies maximize producer surplus and thus increase the value of the platform.

One way of countering this would be for governments or states themselves to build platforms, or nationalize existing platforms to maximize public benefit. However, possible tendencies towards abuse would exist in this case as well. Compared with the monopolistic platforms, no economic benefits might ensue. Irrespective of this, the data harvested on the platforms could still be used to influence the voting behavior of citizens or discriminate against them. Nevertheless, nationalization is almost impossible, not least because of the international nature of platforms—and equally the legal principles for such an undertaking do not exist.

SHAPING THE FUTURE TOGETHER

Platform capitalism continues to expand, but this is not yet the end of the story. Indeed, platforms will dominate in all industries, even though we are still in the early stages, at least in the industrial sector. Society, state, regulators, and operators must work together towards sustainable solutions. Through the triumph of the platforms and exponential developments in the use of artificial intelligence, the way we work in particular is changing. The essence of modern societies is thus facing a revolution that will bring many positive things, but which also involves considerable challenges.

Notes

1. Bloomberg, 26.11.2018. Apple: 721 billion Euros; Google (Alphabet): 589 billion Euros; Microsoft: 698 billion Euros; Amazon: 649 billion Euros; Facebook: 334 billion Euros; Alibaba: 339 billion Euros; Tencent: 311 billion Euros.

2. Eurostat, 2017.

3. Cf. in part, Dr. Sebastian von Engelhardt, Dr. Leo Wangler, and Dr. Steffen Wischmann, *Eigenschaften und Erfolgsfaktoren digitaler Plattformen – Eine Studie im Rahmen der Begleitforschung des Technologieprogramms AUTONOMIK für Industrie 4.0 des Bundesministeriums für Wirtschaft und Energie*, 2017.

4. Cf. Nick Srnicek, *Platform Capitalism* (Cambridge: Polity, 2016), pp. 50f.

5. Cf. ibid., 62ff.

6. Cf. ibid., 71ff.

7. Cf. ibid., 75ff.

8. Cf. ibid., 67ff.

9. Cf. Wu Youyou, Michal Kosinski, and David Stillwell, "Computer-based Personality Judgments are More Accurate than those made by Humans" in *Proceedings of the National Academy of Sciences*, 112 (4), 2015, pp. 1036–1040.

CHAPTER 16

A VISION FOR THE FUTURE OF CAPITALISM

CHRISTOPH G. PAULUS

In this essay, it is assumed that capitalism will develop and will not be replaced by any kind of alternative form of economic activity. Based on this premise, first of all we will discuss possible lines of development (section A), before then sketching out a vision (section B). While the first section attempts to focus as closely as possible on current conditions in order to conceive of the future scenario as realistically as possible, the second section will focus more on what is desirable than what is probable. This is the necessary consequence of our self-imposed topic: visions must inevitably prioritize the "ought" over the "is."

A. SCENARIOS FOR DEVELOPMENT

Concentrations—in legal terms, cartels or monopolies—are on the rise. Commercial enterprises aspire to absolute power such as we only really encounter historically in political entities like the Roman Empire, the Mongols under Genghis Khan, or more recently, the USA, and China with its "New Silk Road" project. Of course, it was often financiers such as the Fuggers or the Welsers and business enterprises like the British East India Company that lay behind such desires for the expansion of power. But today, it would at least seem that such extra-governmental aspirations are much more open, more widespread, and more aggressive than ever before. A few examples should suffice to make this clear.

Market platforms such as eBay or wholesale businesses such as Amazon are conquering literally the whole world, and expanding their business operations into private households. The pervasive phenomenon of "Alexa"—that is, the agent of desired goods located in the one's own home (*de facto*, the device is nothing more than a branch of Amazon's mega-business in one's own living room, which the customer actually has to pay for instead of charging Amazon rent)—is nothing more than an outsourced salesperson in one's own living room. As is well known, the consequences are serious: if a child, interviewed on breakfast television, tells the interviewer how "Alexa" has surprisingly fulfilled her desire for a dollhouse, this leads to "Alexa" delivering this dollhouse to all the households who have been watching this interview as well. Elsewhere, it is reported that a talking parrot almost ruined its owner, because it repeated "orders" over and over again.

While such stories might still be passed off as entertaining curiosities, other implications are much more serious for the way we live as a society. We need only think about how the retail trade has been marginalized. Many of today's relatively small stores have had to close because customers only frequent them not to buy the desired object, for example, but to visualize it concretely and hold it in their hands before ordering it afterwards at home via the Internet and having it delivered by parcel service. Or the Internet of Things means that the refrigerator orders more milk or butter by itself, because a smart contract has identified that supplies are running low. The gradual disappearance of stores means that the streets are becoming wastelands, where little more than cafés or offices can survive. This desertification of the streets, however, leads to the retreat of life from the public sphere and its relocation to other spaces—wherever they might exist outside the individual's own home.

Once again, we might want to regard and justify this scenario as merely an all-too-human withdrawal into one's own comfort zone; but more of a threat are commercial enterprises' aspirations to globalization in other areas. And we are not even talking about when the aforementioned platforms reach such a size that they can earn money even when their customers return the goods they ordered, which consumer protection law readily allows them to do. To enable this, companies such as Amazon, eBay, and their Chinese equivalents only have to acquire the logistics companies that deliver or pick up the goods from the customer. Once you have reached this size, you are on the way to fulfilling an old dream of humankind—the creation of a perpetual motion machine, that is, a set of instruments that carries on working, or in this instance creating money, by itself.

No, the danger really begins when companies start to use the law to gain advantages and special status unilaterally. We can make sense of this through an initial, general observation. Like almost all the works of humankind, the law is both a blessing and a curse. Always and everywhere, the law has been used to gain, consolidate, and reinforce power. The law can be used to repress; the exercise of the law can constitute the greatest injustice: *summum ius, summa iniuria*. Fighting, as it were, against this aspect of law is the other aspect, which uses the law to protect the weak. In the opening passage of the famous Code of Hammurabi of around 1750 BCE, the Babylonian King Hammurabi boasted that he was passing this law to protect the weak and those in need. Lawmakers before him, and many others after him, have pursued similar concerns. Thus, the law has something of a dual function; it can be both weapon and defense.

On the basis of this insight into the nature of the law, a not inconsiderable feeling of anxiety creeps up on the observer, when he realizes that whole sectors of industry are lobbying massively to ensure that laws applicable—in theory—to everyone are not to be applied to them, and that instead they are accorded a privileged position. Two examples demonstrate this in the field of the (only *prima facie* marginal) law of insolvency.

First, there is the so-called Cape Town Convention. It came about because the aircraft industry quite understandably instigated legal proceedings, saying that due to the mobile nature of their products, which was inevitable as a result of their purpose, a legally consistent scope for planning was impossible; after all, each time a border was crossed, the legal situation changed. In order to be able to provide this situation with some guarantees that were at least incontestable, i.e. enforceable in the event of insolvency, the Convention creates a globally insolvency-proof interest, even if the local demands for an insolvency-proof guarantee are not met. What sounds completely reasonable up to this point becomes worrying when we look at the process of the Convention's creation and its implications. Not only did the drafting of the Convention take place subject to the considerable influence of Airbus and Boeing's lawyers; now, other sectors of industry have also obtained equivalent privileges under the umbrella of the Convention—whether directly or by the back door. In other words, whole industrial sectors are unshackling themselves from the generally binding legal framework and gaining special advantages.

Almost more clearly than in the case of the Cape Town Convention, this is evident in the financial sector. As of today, in 80 jurisdictions, this sector has managed to secure privileges that reduce their risk of insolvency in certain transactions to virtually zero. In an almost classic example, we can see that the granting of this privileged status has led to a typical moral hazard, that is, to the kind of extremely reckless behavior that contributed significantly to the recent financial crisis (2007–09). This is particularly cynical because the demand for the introduction of these privileges at that time was based on the idea that systemic crises might otherwise be triggered. Now, these self-same privileges have meant that for more than ten years since then banking supervision worldwide has been trying to prevent the systemic threat posed by exactly the same financial crises as the previous one.

There are surely many more examples of such distortions in equality, where lobbying leads to massive inequalities in legal treatment—and thus to shifts in power. However, we can let the matter rest for the moment, because there exists an even more dangerous version of gaining unilateral advantage in legal matters, one which has not yet really come to general attention, in Germany at least. This version bears the threat potential in its very name—the *weaponization* of financial instruments. What exactly is meant by such a transformation of loan agreements into weapons is, inherently, unknown; endeavors of this kind—and they have probably existed under this designation since the early 1990s—are not brought out into the public sphere, but are worked on out of sight in secret. Thus we have to rely on speculation if we want to reconstruct them.

A strategy practiced and debated in the USA under the name "loan-to-own" might be a quite appropriate reconstruction. This strategy allows an external company to be taken over using terms of contract, without having to observe the strict provisions of takeover law that ensure fair compensation. The rights granted to the creditors by these terms of contract are used—like a weapon—as a lever to take control of the company, under threat or even implementation of insolvency proceedings. And thus the "war" has been won and new territory gained. Although this is openly debated in the USA and is indeed known *de facto* in Germany—ThyssenKrupp is currently the probable object or victim of such a process—remarkably it has not yet been recognized as a coherent strategy, at least not among a wider public.

Even if we were inclined to regard these shark-like attitudes as an acceptable new feature of economic life, it would be extremely dangerous if this economic model were transferred to government loan agreements. This is by no means an abstract worst-case scenario, rather there are indications that not only is this idea being considered, but it is actually being implemented in practice. Instead of military attacks, contractually agreed options are used, for example, to disconnect the debtor state from the capital market, thereby inducing its insolvency, and thus bringing about all the chaotic domestic conditions that have now been well documented by media reports and television images from Argentina, Greece, Ukraine, and many other countries in a comparable situation. In those kinds of situations where, for example, healthcare is drastically decreasing in proportion to the increase in demand, it is enough for the creditor state to offer a consignment of doctors and medication—if the all-important signature is written on the "victor's document."

In summary, we can see from the crescendo of horrors described here that capitalism has at least a tendency to use and design legal instruments (thus far considered innocuous) in such a way that reminds us of all the historic power struggles between countries. The age-old goals of monopolizing power are pursued using ever more sophisticated methods.

B. VISIONS

In view of the last observation, it is absolutely essential to offer a vision—it should, of course, be sufficiently realistic that it is not to be considered as a case for hospitalization—that shows a way in which the threat potential described might be contained. In other words, the good aspect of the law must recapture the territory that is slipping from its grasp.

If we look around the world today, we can see, in overly simplistic terms, three models for dealing with these developments. On the one hand there is the revitalization of selfishness with its most prominent trailblazer, the USA and its policy of "America First." Experience at least suggests that this does not offer a real way forward, because, among other things, it opens the floodgates to capitalist competition and thus fuels rather than limits the worst-case scenario described above.

The second model is exemplified by China with its total control of the population through "social screening." This seems to be the direct realization of the situation so superbly described by Aldous Huxley in *Brave New World*, a world that is divided into Alpha, Beta, and Gamma castes. In China, everything, including the capitalist behavior of entrepreneurs, is centrally controlled, thereby fundamentally contradicting all the ideas of freedom of the individual that have developed in the West over recent centuries.

There then comes the third model: Europe. And this is where the vision starts. Europe must continue its tradition and create capitalism with a human face. This means that the income gap should not become too wide, the welfare state must be strengthened rather than merely maintained, and that the fundamentally European characteristic of "unity in diversity" should be increasingly emphasized. Of course, all that is easy to say, but difficult to put into practice. If, for example, in Industry 4.0 artificial intelligence makes entire professions disappear and thus cuts off armies of citizens from work and income opportunities, an ever-growing precariat will arise in the shape of those who have neither the intellectual nor the material capabilities to keep pace with these innovations or even find new professions. At the same time, this is a massive threat to democracy, because democracy depends on the existence and stability of a large middle class. If the aforementioned precariat threatens this middle class, a threat arises that we can see happening almost in real time today, namely the rejection of democracy.

What may help in the context of this scenario is the totally unconditional investment in education. The ever more ingenious methods we mentioned above, used by those giving themselves one-sided advantages, must be stopped. This requires education on a large scale, and a commitment to knowledge. Knowledge and information are generally considered the crude oil of the 21st century. Just as the car went from a dream to a reality for everyone in the 20th century, knowledge and education for all must become the universal program of European politics in our century.

CHAPTER 17

THE PLAGUE OF STABILITY: WHAT PREVENTS US FROM HAVING VISIONS OF THE FUTURE?

HANS ULRICH OBRIST AND ADAM CURTIS IN CONVERSATION

An edited transcript of a conversation between Hans Ulrich Obrist and Adam Curtis at the Convoco Forum on July 28, 2018, in Salzburg

Hans Ulrich Obrist: Every year, Corinne and I discuss who could be the artist or filmmaker at Convoco. When Corinne rang me this time, she mentioned the theme "The Multiple Futures of Capitalism." The first thing that came to my mind was a story the late

Christoph Schlingensief, the amazing theater director, artist, politician, and activist, once told me. He was born at the beginning of the 1960s and grew up in the German town of Oberhausen as the son of pharmacists. His parents were members of the local Rotary Club. One day, his father came home from the Rotary Club and said that an artist called Joseph Beuys had given a lecture. That was in the 1970s. Beuys predicted that somehow towards the end of the 20th century or the beginning of the 21st century, capitalism would end. And what is interesting is that Christoph was so impressed that his father was destabilized and talked about that for so many weeks that he thought there must be a power in art. And that is the day he decided to become an artist. Christoph told me that the very first time we met. I always thought this was a wonderful story.

What also came to my mind, when Corinne called, was my professor, the late Hans Christoph Binswanger at the University in St. Gallen. I studied with him at the end of the 1980s. Binswanger directed the University of St. Gallen's Institute for Economics and Ecology, teaching the relationship between economics, ecology, and also alchemy. He wrote an amazing book on money and magic in which he traced the deep associations between these different fields. He specialized in the idea of growth limits, and how we can only survive if we introduce ecology into the equation of future economies. He always told me about Johann Wolfgang von Goethe and how this great writer was, at a certain moment in his political career, very involved in economic decisions as a minister [of state in the republic of Weimar].

That leads us to something that is extremely interesting if we talk about the future: the involvement of artists at the center of society, and the involvement of artists in discussions about the future. The future not only of art but of society—which is why it's so wonderful that Corinne invites an artist or a filmmaker to each Convoco conference. Last year, Hito Steyerl joined Convoco in Berlin for a conversation about artificial intelligence. In London in the 1960s, John Latham and Barbara Steveni founded the organization called the Artist Placement Group. They said that every company, every ministry, every corporation should have an artist-in-residence. I think that's still an important idea, and we should somehow try to implement that in the 21st century.

And now, I would like to come to Adam. Adam Curtis of course needs no introduction. His films have been seen by millions of people all over the world. You can watch them on YouTube—they are all online. Since

1983, Adam has been working on films within the BBC, using BBC archival footage. Power is very often the theme of these films—power and how it works in society. I would like to mention some of the films here: *The Power of Nightmares: The Rise of the Politics of Fear* (2004), *All Watched Over by Machines of Loving Grace* (2011), and *The Century of the Self* (2002). We are going to talk about the latter later on in relation to our theme, as well as, of course, *HyperNormalisation* (2016), which is his most recent film. Before I start with my first questions, Adam wanted to begin with a few observations and reactions to the previous Convoco panels on the theme of "The Multiple Futures of Capitalism" that took place this afternoon.

Adam Curtis: Thank you. I am a journalist. I am not an artist, I am a journalist. And what journalists are really good at—it's the only thing they're really good at, everything else they are really bad at—is going out and finding out what people think and feel. What I was slightly shocked about this afternoon was that no one on the panels mentioned the people and what the people think about capitalism—really. They are the people that you are running this system in the name of. That's your job. Your job is to make that system actually work for the people, and I wanted to tell you that you have got a really serious problem. I don't think you are really facing up to it in any of the conversations you had here this afternoon. In my country, the UK, and in the US, which is really what I can talk about, the people—and we're not just talking about what Mrs. Hillary Clinton called "the deplorables" but also large numbers of people—think that capitalism gives them no future, may not even be capitalism any longer, may have mutated into something else, but certainly is not in their interest.

It started with the Iraq War, when those in charge—the think tanks, the politicians, the journalists—lied to the population and led them into a bloody war, which then led indirectly and directly to the refugee crisis you now have, which no one knows how to solve. Then there was a financial crisis in which what we might call "skimming and rigging" was shown to be happening on a very large scale in the US and Britain, and no one was prosecuted. No one high up was prosecuted. No one was sent to jail. And now we live in a world where the people—millions of people—borrow fantastic amounts of money from the banks to buy a small apartment. They will never be able to pay it back. The apartment is so far outside the city that they have to spend the rest of their income on transport. So sometimes, they can't even buy themselves lunch. I am not just talking about poor people. I am talking about people who work in my organization, the BBC, who cannot afford lunch sometimes because they have given all that money to the banks and spent it on transport, because their apartment is now in zone 6 because the property prices are so high. The only lunch they have is on Mondays, when Starbucks does half-price vouchers. They look forward to that. These are middle-class people. There is real anger. What they ask themselves is, what is this all for?

I was brought up to believe that democracy and capitalism were intimately linked. We gave you our vote so you would take us somewhere that would make life better for us. That link seems to have broken in the minds of millions and millions of people in the UK and the US. I am slightly shocked that you didn't mention it—any of that view. This is going to cause you real problems unless you address it, because if we don't know what something is for, we are going to turn to someone else who is going to tell us stories about what it is for, and it ain't capitalism, I can tell you that.

That was my main observation. I think you are all very clever and much cleverer than I am, but knowing all this stuff, I wanted to report to you as a journalist what the people feel—that capitalism gives them no future. None. Zero. Because it no longer tells them a story about where they are going. What is it all for? That is my little rant over!

HUO: This is very interesting, because it reminds me of something Studs Terkel always told me. Like you, as a great historian and as a journalist, he has basically done over 5,000 interviews. He always told me we had to listen. Last week, I was with Etel Adnan—the amazing poet and painter who lives in Paris—who is now in her 90s. Etel said the 20th century had all been about manifestos, often very loud manifestos, and maybe in the 21st century we should listen more. This notion of listening seems to be very important. I wanted to ask you to talk about visions, because we gave this panel the theme of visions. You often say that there is a lack of vision of the future. Of course there is a problem in society when there is no vision for the future. Fernand Braudel talked about *la longue durée*, "the long duration." At the beginning of the 19th century, there were already lots of ideas about what the 20th century could be. Last year, we did research on visions for the next century, the 22nd century, and there is a real lack of such visions. So I wanted to ask you to tell us about that and maybe also about when you think we stopped having visions.

AC: 1992, I think. The last great politician was Margaret Thatcher, because she bought into the idea of Friedrich von Hayek, the Austrian economist, that you cannot impose your vision on millions of other people because it ends up being a totalitarian force. This is what von Hayek's book *The Road to Serfdom* (1944) was all about. Mrs. Thatcher had an ideological vision that she was going to create a society where it was going to be impossible to enforce other people's visions on each other, a society where everyone had their own vision. It is called individualism. This was the politics of individualism, and she did it beautifully. But she then left the scene rather grumpily in 1992, and her successors were faced with a society in which by definition you were not allowed to take people anywhere else. You had become a manager. I lived through this and was a journalist during that time. Politicians were puzzled that the old contract they had, which was "you give me your vote, and I will take you somewhere," didn't work any longer because you had to have a political party to do that, to give you power, and no one wanted to join a party any longer. They wanted to be individuals. And good for them! It is really empowering to be an individual, but it screwed up mass democracy. Mass democracy and individualism just doesn't work because it is like herding piglets. They are not all going to vote for you. So you end up by giving up being the representatives of those in power—which is the old idea of democracy—and you switch and become their managers. That worked very well for about 16 years because you used the money to lend to people. Their wages seemed to go up. They could buy what they wanted, and everything was perfect. But what that system doesn't allow for is crisis, and you had a crisis, and that is when the politicians got puzzled.

I always maintain that if only my government and the government in the US had put 50 bankers into jail in each country in 2008, we wouldn't have got Brexit and we wouldn't have got Trump. It would have been seen by the electorate as an exercise of power in the interests of the people. But they didn't do it. They let it get away, and they didn't punish anyone. At that point a switch went in people's minds, which said "these aren't really politicians any longer. These are just sort of managers." And whenever they say there is a crisis, everyone goes on, "oh it's terrible," and then nothing happens. That is what people have got used to. At that point—starting in 1992—and later, when we began to realize in 2008/09 that they weren't going to do anything to change things when they got bad, we knew that they have no idea of the future. None. And that is where we are now.

HUO: In your film, *HyperNormalisation*, you actually go back earlier than 1992. You talk about something that happened in the 1970s, because you said that in the 1970s there was a shift wherein self-expression became the new politics—self-expression as a way of seeing the world. Could you talk a little bit about that?

AC: This is the issue that I always get in trouble about, because it involves an attack on art. Listening to economists, it seems to me that they are very nice people. When you attack artists, they are not nice, they are really horrible. They have a go at you. What I was questioning was this: if you try to do radical art, whatever you say, however radical your message is, in a world driven by individualism in which Nike wants to sell you sneakers so you can "express yourself better," and all products are there to help you express yourself better, you are feeding the very beast that you are trying to destroy. You are making it stronger, because you are reinforcing the idea of self-expression in people's minds.

The most radical thing you could do today is to do something extraordinary and not tell anyone you have done it—not write a book about it, not put it on Instagram, not tell your friends. Just do something really, really extraordinary and then not let anyone know you have done it. That would be much more radical than anything anyone could do. Which brings us back to the peculiar idea that self-expression, which was born out of the radical ideas of the 1960s, has now become the conformity of our time.

In terms of the exercise of power, it is brilliant that this self-expression is actually quite disempowering when really bad things happen. It is great to be self-expressive when things are going really well, but when something goes really badly wrong and you are left alone, expressing yourself in a tweet in big capital letters is not a very strong thing to do, so you feel very lonely. I wonder whether this conformity is now actually not only just to keep people stable but actually to disempower them a bit.

The most radical thing is to go back to the old ideas of politics, which is that you join together with lots of other people. You sacrifice quite a lot of your own self-expression and your own self-satisfaction for other people. To go back to what Adam Smith said right at the beginning about the whole idea of morals, it's central to his idea of capitalism. It's not just about the market. It's about you having the capacity and wanting to think about how other people feel and how possibly you could make them feel better. And maybe that is what is coming, and that is maybe what is going to rescue capitalism, but I am not sure.

HUO: You gave the film the title *HyperNormalisation*, which comes from a 2006 book about the final decade of the Soviet Union: *Everything Was Forever, Until It Was No More.* Can you tell us about how you found the title—because it is interesting in relation to this conversation—and also a little bit more about *HyperNormalisation*? It would also be interesting to hear about risk-adversity, because last time we met, you talked about it, and I was wondering where you see that coming from. Also, how can we supersede this risk-adversity?

AC: It is a really good book. I recommend it to everyone. It is written by Alexei Yurchak [professor of anthropology at the University of California, Berkeley]. It is a history of the collapse of the Soviet Union during the 1980s, told at the level of what I was talking about earlier—how people felt. It is about what it felt like to live through that collapse from about 1983 through to 1991. Yurchak coins the phrase "hypernormalisation" in this book to describe what it felt like. What is so important when you are discussing the future of capitalism—or the future of anything—is what it feels like for the millions of people, because what then happens depends upon them. He described what it felt like to live through the collapse of the Soviet Union when everyone knew that all those in power were corrupt: the managers of the state plan were corrupt, the technocrats above them running the whole thing, the whole apparatus of administration, and the politicians in power. All were corrupt. But not only that: everyone knew that they had no idea of an alternative. They were stuck. So everyone was living through this world that they knew was sort of wrong, but because no one at any level had any other idea, they just accepted it as normal. And what Yurchak coined was this phrase, which I think is just brilliant. He called it "hypernormalisation." You knew that it was all wrong, but because no one was giving you any alternative, you just went along with it, telling yourself: "That is normal."

In my film, I argued that, although in Britain and the US we are not at all like the Soviet Union, in many ways we are living through that same slow-motion, strange world. In the UK, everyone knows that those in power accept the corruption and don't do anything about it. And it happens again and again and again. Endless stories of corruption come out in the newspapers. The journalists make a great fuss. Everyone goes on about how wonderful investigative journalism is, and then nothing happens. We also know that those in charge—I include the administrative class of the financial system in this as well—have no idea of an alternative either. And we accept it. So I was arguing in that film that we are pretty hypernormal at the moment, and we are just waiting to see what happens because we know that the people in charge don't know anything. Nothing.

Look at what is happening with Brexit in the UK: nothing. I mean, it is funny, but that is it. They have no idea. But there is this whole apparatus of think tanks—I blame the think tanks, they are the really bad ones—that have to pretend that everyone talking about Brexit knows what they are talking about. I don't know if any of you have ever read Charles Dickens' novel *Bleak House.* The central plot is a law case called Jarndyce v. Jarndyce. No one can remember what this case is about, and that is what Brexit is like. No one can actually remember the arguments, but there is a whole apparatus that has to pretend that they do. But we know that they are pretending, and they know that we know that they are pretending. It really is like that, and that is very strange. In a way, it is a work of high art that you have got all these so-called clever, highly educated people, who have managed to create this apparatus that is lifting off the ground, and no one can remember what it is about. That is really great—not because it actually could lead to tragic consequences, but because it is absurd. That is what I am really trying to say. Politics and the administrative class just cannot deal with absurdity at the moment. What we are waiting for is a politician who can deal with absurdity, who can bring that absurdity forward, make us look at it and say: this is what is happening, we will use this, and we will go elsewhere. But at the moment we haven't got one.

HUO: It is fascinating that you mention Dickens' book. I was thinking this morning what the novels about Brexit are. Ali Smith's book *Autumn* (2016) is a great first attempt at writing the Brexit novel.

When we met for the first time, maybe seven or eight years ago, we organized a retrospective of your works together with Liam Gillick at the platform e-flux. You agreed to do the exhibition only under one condition, which is that I wouldn't call you an artist. We agreed on that and called you a journalist and documentary filmmaker. But it was interesting that in that first conversation at the time, I asked you who were your heroes or heroines—the most important people who inspired you—and you immediately answered Max Weber. Weber wrote about an "iron cage" of efficiency, and the idea of how we can break out of this cage. So, in relation to *HyperNormalisation*,

I was wondering if you could tell us a little bit about why Max Weber is so important, and how you think we can go beyond the current state of managerialism. You have already alluded to it, but I'd like to hear more in terms of a to-do list. What can we do?

AC: Weber is fascinating because he anticipated the rise of bureaucracy and the managerial system and its constant attempts to take power away from politics and hold it stable and static, and I think he got there before anyone else. The "iron cage" of rationality, which is what he is talking about, is fascinating. Somewhere, politics got captured by economics, and economic rationality has now colonized the whole of politics. I think that happened in 1992, by the way. Economics has a very powerful role to play in politics and a very good role. But when the politicians gave up their old idea of representing us and became managers, they embraced a utilitarian philosophy, namely that you can measure outcomes, you want to achieve stability, and that is your job.

You were talking about risk. I did a search—it is not brilliantly scientific, but on LexisNexis—of the use of the words "risk" and "stability." It really only starts— guess when?—in 1992. That is when the word "risk" starts to be used. Again, I think it is part of this shift in politics. You went from the idea of being part of a dynamic process of history that took the people some-where—and that's what Mrs. Thatcher thought too, that she was taking the people somewhere—to giving that up, and instead you go for a static, managed model of the world where your job is to keep things stable. As a politician, you don't take risks any longer, because you know that ideologically, very deep in people's brains, you will get massacred if something bad happens. So what you are is a manager. Therefore, risk becomes the sort of thing you must hold on to.

I think that is dangerous, because while that works in a technical area of economic management and risk planning for all sorts of industrial things, if you're a leader of human beings—of the people—and you say, my job is to keep you safe and to keep you stable, what happens to your imagination is this: you give up imagining good things in the future, which is what the old politics used to do—including right-wing poli-tics. Both sides imagined good things, and they said, I will take you there. If you are saying, I am going to keep you safe, you have to imagine the worst. I did a whole series of films about what happened after 9/11, the hysteria about the apocalyptic vision that was coming our way because of terrorism. I noticed that if you have to imagine what could happen, your imagination knows no bounds. You start imagining very dark things. I think that is also what happened to politics especially in the UK. The politicians started to imagine the worst. And when that spreads through a society, that infects not only the imagination of the politicians, but the imagination of everyone else as well. And everyone becomes frightened. I don't know about your society, but in my society, the thing that is humming away in the back of people's minds is "Oh God, what is going to happen next." There is that fear; it sits there; it hums away. This is because we gave up the idea that we can be strong together, that we can go forward into the future, and we replaced it with the idea that "we are going to stay where we are, stable, and we are going to protect you against the darkness." I don't think that is a very good place for politicians to be. Because when really difficult things happen, such as the financial crisis of 2008, you don't know what to do, because you haven't got an alternative. As I said earlier on, it is hypernormal and you just live with it. And meanwhile everyone is a little bit jangly. The mood in the UK is jangly. It is nervous. Everyone feels just slightly insecure. Not terrified, just slightly inse-cure. There is no administrative class that understands how to deal with that. But there are people coming who do know how to deal with that. They tell you big, dramatic stories that sweep you up and stop that jangly feeling and make you feel part of something big. But they are not democrats. Unless you pull yourself together, they are the people that are going to come and grab you and stop that jangly feeling and make you feel big. You know it is coming, it really is.

HUO: In my introduction, I mentioned Joseph Beuys, the protagonist of social sculpture. There is a great interest right now among many younger artists in this area of social sculpture. One of the ways to address the things you have been describing is the idea of transcending oneself and joining together with other people. You talked about that in our previous interview. You said: "If a novelist is going to come along and write a grand novel of our time, I think the sensibility will have to deal with the interaction between the desire of the individual to feel and experience everything themselves and how that desire can transcend the immediacy." So, two last questions. One question is: how can the idea of the collective be reconciled with the commitment to individualism? How do you see that?

AC: This is the big problem. If you live in a world of individualism, how do you get people back together again into a collective group to actually use that power creatively? How do you get people to surrender some of their individualism for something good when they just want to be individuals? I know it myself; I don't want to join a political party. I want to be an individual. That is the thing of our time. When the Internet came along, I thought it had squared the circle. Because the Internet is brilliant at letting you feel that you are in control of your own destiny, because you are going wherever you want with your fingers. But actually, it is like a Ouija board, because behind the screen the machines can look at all the patterns that you are making with lots of other people and see that you are actually very similar. The machines agglomerate you together and can actually see you as a group, while you are still feeling you are an individual. When the Internet started, I thought that might be what the Internet was going to do. It was going to be the solution to this problem. It got hijacked somewhere towards the end of the 1990s by these four firms, who are simply using it to advertise stuff to us.

HUO: That brings us to my last question, about blockchain. If we talk about future capitalisms, I want to bring up blockchain. I am doing this research now: at the moment, many artists do projects related to blockchain, for example, Simon Denny, also Matt Liston and Avery Singer. They are creating a blockchain religion. There are also a lot of projects right now that work on new cooperative models across geographies using blockchain with artists. I wanted to ask you your take on that, on the future of blockchain.

AC: They are all talking about blockchain now. I have two problems with blockchain. One is, it is always men that talk to you about blockchain. I have never met a woman who talks about blockchain, so I am a bit suspicious. Before I say what I think is fundamental about blockchain, let me go back to the original question that Mrs. Flick asked right at the beginning: what is the future of capitalism? I'll tell you where capitalism is at the moment. It is at that point where the Catholic Church collapsed and Protestantism came in. It is not that people didn't like religion, but they thought that the Catholic Church had become totally corrupted through practices such as indulgences which you bought as an excuse for not having to really be religious. It had become a completely corrupt system that everyone knew didn't really involve belief any longer. Along came Martin Luther and argued that you should go back to basics. I have a similar feeling about capitalism. Given all the warnings I have been ranting on about, I don't think you are going to get a revolution. I think what you are going to get is people saying, "We want to go back—we want to renew capitalism. Bring the word 'free' back in." Let us go back to Adam Smith and with Adam Smith bring moral sentiment into it. Smith's key point is that you have the free market, which means you have that idea of the freedom of the individual to actually change their own world and be in control of their own destiny. But they are also good people. All this rubbish about people being hard-wired into being greedy—people are not hard-wired into anything. They can be all sorts of things. What Smith was trying to point out in that idea of moral sentiment is that people actually quite like it if they can make other people feel better. If you can combine that with the market, then you have got a beautiful idea. I suspect that might be what will happen to capitalism. I am afraid it might mean that the giant administrative think-tank/industrial conglomerate will get swept away, and what will come back is the idea of the individual connecting—through money, through the market—to their own destiny, which brings me in a roundabout way back to blockchain.

Because that might be what blockchain does. What destroyed the power of the Catholic Church was printing, because they no longer had a monopoly on information and data, although it wasn't called that then. The same may be true with blockchain. It may be a way of reinventing your relationship to money and power—as an individual. You get rid of the hierarchy, like you got rid of the hierarchy in the Catholic Church. The only problem with it is that blockchain doesn't tell you a story. Blockchain is a technocratic boys' thing. It doesn't tell you an emotional story. Similarly, I didn't hear an emotional story this afternoon. You are only going to win the people back if you tell them an emotional story. A really powerful story, which is what Luther did. That is what Protestantism is about: You can connect to God yourself. That is what you are waiting for. But maybe it will come about through blockchain.

CHAPTER 18

THE DOCTRINE OF THE MEASURE
AND MODERATION RELOADED:
A VISIONLESS VISION

TIMO MEYNHARDT

Capitalism will survive if it can continue to create a balance between community [*Gemeinschaft*] and society [*Gesellschaft*] that is acceptable to the majority of people—otherwise it will not. To adapt Lenin, if it is no longer possible to continue and no longer desirable to continue, then something new will emerge.

Above all, people live within families, relationships, and social structures—in short, within their forms of "association" which may be shaped by an economic system, albeit never completely determined.

It is the quality of these forms of association between people that forms the basis of each economic system, and from which it derives its legitimizing power. This is the source of the support needed to make a social system viable in the first place.

Of course, social conditions create the framework for the individual's development, but they are in turn the result of realities relating to the human psyche. Formulated for the first time by Ferdinand Tönnies, one of the founding fathers of modern sociology, the importance of this idea cannot be overestimated: "All social forms are artifacts of psychic substance, and their sociological conceptualization, therefore, must be a psychological conceptualization at the same time."[1] For sociology today "this amounts to the discovery of a forgotten sphere of problems—that social conditions are based on modes of consciousness which, as the embodiment of 'feelings, instincts, and desires,' not only precede rational action genetically but release such action from itself in the first place."[2]

Grounded in sociology, this perspective takes us to the heart of the matter: the future of capitalism in all its varieties (at least the American, Chinese, and European versions) will depend on the extent to which the implementation of its basic principles, in particular free competition, private property, and the principle of the increasing accumulation of capital, has a positive effect on the fulfillment of basic human needs and thus demonstrably contributes to the common good. Every ambitious theory of capitalism needs a concept of the nature of humankind, their "feelings, instincts, and desires," and of how a commonwealth [*Gemeinwesen*] can function on this basis.

Whether we like it or not, it is the psychological, subjective factor that decides whether and to what extent any kind of system transformation takes place or not. In other words, the future of capitalism is not primarily determined in the economic sphere, but by its ability to strengthen social ties within and between groups and/or to create an acceptable balance between them.

Others agree: in January 2018, Larry Fink, Founder, Chairman and CEO of BlackRock, the world's largest asset management company, called on companies to develop a "sense of purpose" and focus their business more towards the benefit of society. However diverse the motives behind this appeal may be, it nevertheless highlights the question voiced ever louder in society concerning the acceptability of the capitalist economic system and the renewed insight that every business operation is inextricably linked to society.

For example, questions about more/less market, more/less digitalization, or more/less globalization, which continue to dominate the debate, acquire their real systemic relevance as they influence the quality of a community's or a society's forms of association. In other words, the future of capitalism will depend on whether it succeeds in emphasizing the human being's basic, anthropological constants that focus on togetherness, solidarity, and empathy.

THE GRAND IDEA OF COMMUNITY AND SOCIETY

Social conditions make different forms of individuality and sociality possible. For example, anyone who wants to understand the interrelationship between "me" and "we," the "we in me," can find many different points of reference in the social sciences. An early example of the positing of socio-psychological theory is Ferdinand Tönnies' work, which influenced almost all the important sociologists in this field during the 20th century.

Tönnies created a body of thought which, although it remains fragmented, is nevertheless very stimulating and groundbreaking when it addresses the question of capitalism's ability to survive. In particular, this is because Tönnies avoids both bias in favor of a rationalist view of the reasoned human being ("society") and the other extreme of an anti-Enlightenment attitude that is skeptical of progress ("community").[3] Above all, by differentiating between *Gemeinschaft* and *Gesellschaft*,[4] Tönnies described fundamental mechanisms whereby people coexist in a commonwealth, mechanisms that can help us today in understanding phenomena such as "social division," "filter bubbles," and "alienation," as well as the emergence of new forms of social bonding. At this point we should note that in each case the plural—communities and civil societies—is also meant. Tönnies uses these nominalizations primarily as a way of succinctly naming different forms of bonding between people.

For Tönnies, one thing is very clear: it is not just rational aspects or logically superior arguments that pertain to the bonding process, but rather and above all, emotions and motivations that resist rationality. The latter do not "convince" by means of argument. As Tönnies put it, it is always "... a positive relationship between these particular sensations and the entire inner state of sensory experience. That inner state is the absolute *a priori*. It can scarcely be imagined except as something embracing within itself the totality of existence in hazy, general relationships, some of which will gradually become clearer through the development and activity of the brain and sense organs, i.e. of the comprehending intellect."[5]

For Tönnies, social structures (as indeed our economy is) are fundamentally influenced by our biological and psychological development.[6] Increasingly nuanced experiential worlds emerge (Tönnies talks about "forms of will") from the system of "feelings, instincts, and desires" that relates to the human psyche and the thinking that takes place within this system. These worlds form the very basis of the forms social relationships take [*Verbundenheiten*, "associations"]. Then, two energizing, complementary mechanisms come into play, mechanisms that do not merely form a whole, but are in a relationship of high tension with each other. The first is indicated by the concept of *community* [*Gemeinschaft*] and designates "real organic life" and thus knowledge derived from the senses, physical experience, and emotional association.

From this emerges the ideal, mechanical construction, described by the concept of *society* [*Gesellschaft*]. As Tönnies writes: "In *Gemeinschaft* we are united from the moment of our birth with our own folk for better or for worse. We go out into *Gesellschaft* as if into a foreign land."[7] Of course, it is a great step forward to break away from the bonds of one's immediate environment. Indeed, the "foreign land" does not necessarily represent a threat (for example, "*Stadtluft macht frei*"*); rather, it is a powerful source of the new.

The systemic power of the community arises from the associations that operate within immediate human relationships (kinship, neighborhood, friendship), where the experiential system of intellectual understanding and emotion is fundamental. In a community, people are essentially interconnected through a system of good/bad customs, everyday reason, or even by "common sense." Common to all these forms of social bond is that they function without any rules or regulations imported from outside.

However, the human mind is able to move beyond immediate sensory experience, and thus as discrimination and reflection increase, new forms of association emerge. They depart from the original system of natural instincts, and later from the intellectual system of thinking and feeling as well. In the course of biological, psychological, and social development, increasingly complex levels of reflection and mental activity interpose themselves between the manifestations of natural existence determined by the senses. The intellectual formation of "concepts," the development of "intentions", and the establishment of "goals" are the products of these new *realities relating to the human psyche* and open up another, new mechanism of association, that of contracts that are entered into consciously and rationally.

As a result, new mental structures are constantly being created, through which new forms of cognition emerge. In this process, the notion of the abstract develops an independent agency, and opens up new options for the way we behave. We can anticipate and think through the consequences of our actions; we can relate hitherto unrelated facts with one another or connect them in new ways. These intellectual achievements are both a *precondition* for the establishment of new social forms and, conversely, are simultaneously underpinned by them.

Thus the essence of society (as opposed to community) lies in the abstract world of rules that is divorced from subjectivity and emotionality, and the resulting formalized relationships of exchange in economic life underlie relationships in the world of trade. In this respect, following Tönnies, the capitalist economic world that relies on the movement of capital is dependent on societalization processes (for example, in the form of a functioning constitutional state). Only the development of formalized social forms (in private law: exchange, contract, and trade; in public law: licenses, prohibitions, levies, etc.) and their economic institutions (culminating in anonymous corporations and state intervention in the economic process) provides a reliable framework for the economy beyond the bounds of community. But even the instrumental rationality of economic action and the calculation of exchange value must also be able to build on the human motivations that underpin them, otherwise credibility and legitimacy will crumble. Economic systems and their operations cannot be explained objectively in themselves, rather they are always the result of "human will" and are to that extent *intentional*.

If we pursue the notion that social conditions are based on modes of consciousness, that they are propelled and made possible by them in the first place, then we come across a possible crisis mechanism: the further the two spheres of community and society drift apart as a result of increasing economic, social, and technical complexity, the harder it is to "understand" what it is all really about. More complexity cannot be managed by superior "explanation" alone; rather, it necessarily and unavoidably entails the creation of meaning through values that are anchored in emotions and motivations. These values then take on a regulatory role, because they allow the essential simplification of complexity and thus focus.

DRIVING THROUGH FOG

In many ways, business leaders often have to behave like car drivers in thick fog—not knowing if they're on the right track, risking a head-on collision with oncoming traffic, and yet driving on nevertheless. Unlike real traffic, in our case there really is no reliable indicator telling us that we are on the wrong track when several hundred vehicles are coming straight at us. This is not a new phenomenon in itself; however, the effects of leverage and speed in technically sophisticated and integrated trading systems and economic cycles do represent something new.

Today, we are confronted with an accumulation of complex situations, and in the world of complexity it seems that many a management intervention resembles a rainmaking dance. We do not like to hear or say this, and yet it cannot be denied: whether economists, sociologists, or psychologists, we are hopelessly out of our depth. The good news is that this condition is chronic, and in a crisis we can see this particularly clearly. And that is why we would do well to proceed both diffidently and modestly in our deliberations and decision-making.

The fact that we are groping in the dark, therefore, is not only attributable to our helplessness, but can be attributed to the nature of our modern societies' (dys)function. By this we mean the trend to transform facts, business relationships, risk assessments, or product ideas into sophisticated, intellectually abstract relationships that we can no longer comprehend—into legal norms, unnecessarily complicated models and theories, which are often almost impossible to translate back into the world of common sense. The magnificent ability of the human mind to use abstraction to move beyond the immediate world of experience quickly turns into complexity, as the (re-) integration into emotions and motivations becomes ever more difficult.

At the beginning, I spoke flamboyantly of a "grand idea." The distinction between community and society, which seems schematic only when regarded superficially, is fundamental because it addresses a central, ambivalent experience of interpersonal life in the modern world in an original way. On the one hand, there are direct, personal relationships in which the individual feels emotionally and motivationally involved and rooted. On the other hand, there are processes that are experienced socially and anonymously as external, unmanageable, and alien—relationships that seem uncontrollable. Despite their differences, both types of association are the result of real developments with their inherent psychological processes, and time after time both have to stand up to a holistic assessment ("inner state of sensory experience").

For Tönnies, it was already obvious that there is no one society/community, but many communities and societies. In contrast to the various labels we use to describe the present, e.g. risk society, leisure society, multi-option society, or knowledge society, Tönnies is concerned with finding answers to the question of how different types of association arise in a social grouping, and how they constantly re-crystallize like chemical elements. It is irrelevant whether these questions are posed in the context of individual "parallel societies" or "virtual communities," for example. At the core there is always the question of how commitment arises in interpersonal relationships.

As he elaborates this idea, Tönnies addresses the often separate spheres of holistic experience and knowledge that requires (re)integration, sometimes anticipating later findings in the field of psychology. The divergence of these spheres through experience and the resulting, constant need for integration are formulated by Tönnies not just at the level of the individual, but as a social problem.

The divergence of community and society produces experiences of alienation ("no longer feeling understood," "social fragmentation," "the world is no longer responsive," etc.). For the sociologist Hartmut Rosa, one solution is to seek out new experiences of "resonance."[8] The sociologist Armin Nassehi, by contrast, advocates improving the way we "handle and use the differentiation of perspective."[9] However, the latter is likely to prove naïve in the context of new demands to tip the balance in favor of community experiences in manageable groups. If the pendulum has swung too far in the direction of a process of societalization that increases complexity, a further increase in the acceptance of perspective can hardly be a recipe for success—as desirable as it may be. The current growth of populist movements that emphasize a focus on community (currently by using concepts such as national identity or homeland in particular), speaks for itself. The challenge is to make legitimate proposals as to how the balance between community and society can be maintained in a tension that is productive and ultimately acceptable to the majority of people.

But it is also possible that viable answers might emerge from capitalism's focus on innovation. Today, the entrepreneurial approach of offering more community-oriented products and services is already producing successful business models—whether it is an emphasis on regionalism in the food industry, community-oriented marketing strategies, and not least ideas about the sharing economy. It is also very much in companies' commercial interest to contribute to sustainable associations through their products and services. But this also applies to the internal organization of the company itself. Here, too, positive simplification is the order of the day, in order to facilitate new forms of association at community level. In this respect, new forms of work (agile, holacratic, etc.) can be seen as attempts to integrate the logic of capitalist production into ever-new forms of communitization, thereby taking account of social needs. Once again, we should remember Larry Fink's abovementioned demand for a *social purpose*, which can also be read as an appeal to develop innovative approaches to promoting associations. For a long time now, practice has shown how entrepreneurs have been trying to make the principle of increasing the accumulation of capital work to create added value for the benefit of the common good.

However, it remains to be seen to what extent the self-transformation of capitalism, which has already begun in a wide variety of areas, will help overcome contradictions, resolve conflicts and, not least, contribute to stability in society. We should be careful about generalizing from particular examples in a complex, unpredictable economic system, and thus encouraging the fantasy that this can be managed. Even Wolfgang Streeck, a prominent and knowledge- able critic of capitalism, admits that the present state of capitalism is still emerging, i.e. "is not necessarily either planned or intended by the actors involved."[10] In a self-organizing system (and there is almost no other way of talking about the capitalist system today), we no longer have an overview.

IN PRAISE OF SMALL STEPS TOWARDS THE COMMON GOOD

To be dependent not only on the goodwill of the local community, but to be able to rely on legal obligations and establish something elsewhere using the abstract medium called "money" is part of what Tönnies means by societalization [*Vergesellschaftung*]. The element of the abstract, that which is detached from an immediate emotional relationship, was originally a great advance in terms of freedom and an engine of progress. However, the phenomena of our current crisis demonstrate that the old balance between the concrete (community) and the abstract (society) has been lost.

This divergence also seems to be the decisive breeding ground for future crises and recurring malfunctions in our economic system. It is only a matter of time before the motor starts faltering again as a result of the highly abstract financial transactions taking place in the interconnected dynamics of our global economy. Those who espouse this perspective conclude that we are not suffering from too much free market economy or too much welfare state. Rather, we are suffering from the logic of excessive societalization, which is inherent to all economic activity, and hence also to modern finance capitalism, and is further intensified by it. It is not so much the pursuit of profit as the systemically integrated abstraction, objectification, and reification of human coexistence, which thus far we have no effective concepts to combat. One thing is clear: a return to "the old days" is not possible.

In these circumstances, three conclusions are conceivable. First, we must muster the strength to stop promoting the extent of societalization in the sense discussed here by using clear but simple rules in the political arena. Or rather: we must create incentives to simplify. We must not trivialize matters, but a further increase in complexity will not solve these problems. If we follow the psychological and sociological argument already discussed, even technical innovations (currently digitalization) are unable to help us, so long as we operate in the abstract space that we cannot occupy emotionally. Second, we must rein in our need to create grand visions. The course of history shows that few things are really predictable—not even in a system that is reasonably manageable. We would therefore do well to give more weight to the "piece-meal approach" as described by the philosopher Karl Popper—small steps, feeling our way, always ready to turn back. We also need to scale back our expectations of politics—it's not just a case of pressing one or two buttons. Our economic system, in all its social inter-dependencies, is far too interconnected for powerful monocausal interventions to threaten overall stability immediately—the unintended side effects are now more important than the intended ones. What should be the focus of decision-makers when everything is so terribly complicated and complex?

The third and most essential consequence is as follows: focus on the common good and judge your actions against their compatibility with the common good! Simply because of the interdependencies within community/society, this imperative is rational. It is but a weak counter-argument to claim that the idea of the common good is antiquated because everyone understands something different by it. Of course, we should always take care that such rhetoric does not—as has happened historically—fuel authoritarian abuse.

But actively contributing to the strengthening of the commonwealth or preventing its damage is the fundamental legitimation of our liberal system. Nothing is more shortsighted than a notion of freedom that does not recognize that unconditional human existence does not exist. The common good should be regarded as a condition of the possibility of a successful life—or to put it more succinctly: "no freedom without the common good." The common good becomes the basic condition of human self-development.

Even if it is hard to bear, our understanding is an obstacle, and we would do well to take its failure into account. Thus, if we want to maintain a free social and economic system, the tendency to abstract business processes and relationships from the immediate conditions of people's lives requires a form of reconnection that is culturally accepted, emotional, and motivational. The common good seems to me to be the most meaningful, historically evolved, regulative idea. In a nutshell, "common sense" has to be rediscovered as a guideline for people's decision-making and action, and criticism is always appropriate when "common sense" is unable to deal with the argument or the solution.

Concentrating on the good feelings that underpin decision-making (I am deliberately not saying "on the good reasons") should become an important asset not only in professional life, but also in primary and secondary education, because it can reinforce the willingness to deal with the associated liberal image of humankind, and can create incentives that reward this. What you cannot do is dictate values or enforce them in a compulsory way.

We should remember that the functioning of a capitalist economic system in which "capital" and "risk" play a decisive role necessarily relies on a focus on the common good. Such a criterion forces a reconciliation between all the productive and destructive forces of abstraction, which make the achievements of the individual forms of capitalism possible in the first place. What we need is a journey of small steps and the courage to simplify things. Without such an emphasis on "the doctrine of the measure and moderation" (Wilhelm Röpke),[11] the viability of the social system is at stake. Focusing on the common good provides a compass that never abandons the experience of community unilaterally to the detriment of the experience of society and vice versa, and always looks for the productive link between the two. It is thus of central importance not to base our hopes on harmony, but to acknowledge this dualism and use the indissoluble relationship of tension creatively.

TOWARDS A VISIONLESS VISION

Capitalism's "condition for survival" as formulated is profoundly focused on the idea of compatibility with the common good. Innovations are required time and again to continue to ensure an equitable balance between community and society. Using the ideas of Ferdinand Tönnies we have an explanatory approach that sums up the capitalist mode of production's dependence on focusing on the common good. Above all, however, it demonstrates the starting point whereby companies today can maintain or increase their acceptability among the population.

However, given the self-organizing nature of complex systems, any kind of vision is doomed to failure from the very beginning if it sets out to be a grand plan. In line with the aforementioned "piece-meal approach," it is important to experiment with new forms of association and discover viable solutions. Indeed, the "muddling through" this creates is not a weakness, but an admission of the complexity generated by us humans.

This does not mean a rejection of individual goals and visions of the future, which give power and direction to the individual, and serve as their vital impetus. Equally, visionless vision does not mean a lack of vision. Rather, the term aims at the preparedness to relentlessly face up to the limitations of individual agency and, at the same time, to focus again and again on the greater good. Living this apparent contradiction might begin by recognizing and accepting the contradiction as a real challenge in the first place.

The associated aspiration to creation and action of individual actors is thus characterized by modesty and humility, as has been recommended since the time of the Stoics: to calmly focus only on those things that one can really change and tackle them courageously. This too is perhaps the core of a visionless vision, which sets its sights on viable forms of association that will benefit the common good and does not let itself be seduced by empty promises of the future. If capitalism aspires to this in such a way, it has a chance of survival.

Notes

* [Translator's note.] *Stadtluft macht frei* [city air makes you free] refers to a German medieval legal principle, whereby serfs were deemed free of their former masters' ownership if they succeeded in living for one year and a day in the city.

1. Ferdinand Tönnies, *On Sociology: Pure, Applied, and Empirical*, ed. with an Introduction by Werner J. Cahnman and Rudolf Heberle (Chicago and London: The University of Chicago Press, 1971), p. 35.

2. Peter-Ulrich Merz-Benz, *Tiefsinn und Scharfsinn. Ferdinand Tönnies' begriffliche Konstitution der Sozialwelt* (Frankfurt am Main: Suhrkamp, 1995).

3. Cornelius Bickel, *Ferdinand Tönnies. Soziologie als skeptische Aufklärung zwischen Historismus und Rationalismus* (Opladen: Verlag für Sozialwissenschaften, 1991).

4. Tönnies, *On Sociology: Pure, Applied, and Empirical*, p. 35.

5. Ferdinand Tönnies, *Community and Civil Society*, ed. Jose Harris, trans. Jose Harris and Margaret Hollis (Cambridge: University of Cambridge Press, 2001), p. 4.

6. The following parts of this essay refer to Timo Meynhardt's chapter, "Management zwischen Main Street und Wall Street" in Timo Meynhardt and Sascha Spoun (eds.), *Management – eine gesellschaftliche Aufgabe* (Baden-Baden: Nomos Verlagsgesellschaft, 2010), pp. 19–45 and Timo Meynhardt's essay, "Mass und Mitte" in *Schweizer Monat* 1000, October 2012, pp. 73–78.

7. Tönnies, *Community and Civil Society*, p. 18.

8. Hartmut Rosa, *Resonance: A Sociology of our Relationship to the World*, trans. James Wagner (Cambridge: Polity, 2019, forthcoming).

9. Armin Nassehi, *Die letzte Stunde der Wahrheit. Kritik der komplexitätsvergessenen Vernunft* (Hamburg: kursbuch edition, 2017), p. 209.

10. Wolfgang Streeck, *Gekaufte Zeit: Die vertagte Krise des demokratischen Kapitalismus* (Berlin: Suhrkamp, 2017), p. 20.

11. Wilhelm Röpke, *Maß und Mitte* (Erlenbach: Eugen Rentsch Verlag, 1950).

CHAPTER 19

EXPECTATIONS AND IMAGINARIES IN THE CAPITALIST ECONOMY

IN CONVERSATION WITH JENS BECKERT

Convoco: In 2018, Convoco is discussing the topic "The Multiple Futures of Capitalism," with the aim of imagining the possible forms capitalism might take in the future. It is easier to invent the future than to predict it, and it is through visions that we invent the future. You have written a book examining to what extent "imaginaries" of the economic future contribute to the dynamics of capitalism. You talk about images of the future. What are "imaginaries" of the future?

Jens Beckert: The future only exists as an idea, as logically there can be no future facts. However, such ideas are enormously important for the way we act in the present. For example, we envisage that the Earth's climate will warm by more than two degrees if we don't reduce CO_2 emissions. This idea underpins current measures being implemented in climate change policy. Or we envisage what it might be like to finally have a certain consumer product—whether it's a new iPhone or a particular pair of shoes. This imaginary motivates our actions. Imaginaries of the future are decisive in all areas of society.

C: You quote the words of St. Augustine of Hippo: "The present of future things is expectations." What effect do expectations have?

JB: Expectations fuel our modern capitalist economy. Actors—whether they are entrepreneurs, investors, or consumers—make decisions with regard to future outcomes, and in this way expectations guide actions. It is characteristic of the modern economy that the future is seen as open and unpredictable but at the same time as able to be influenced. Under these conditions, expectations are imaginaries of a future world, whose realization is dependent on actions in the present. Whether they actually are realized, however, cannot be foreseen.

C: You talk about "fictional expectations." What do you mean by this?

JB: Actors imagine what the present will be in the future and build their expectations upon it. Investment in electromobility, for example, is based on the idea that electrically driven vehicles will replace the internal combustion engine. But no one can predict whether this will in fact happen. Investment in Tesla shares might be a goldmine or an unfounded speculative exaggeration. By investing, however, we behave *as if* the future will change in the imagined way. This *as if* applies both to expectations under conditions of uncertainty and to fictional texts. The author of a novel behaves *as if* the action described might actually take place or has taken place. It is in this sense that I talk about fictional expectations.

C: Is uncertainty one of the cornerstones of capitalism?

JB: The dynamics of capitalism are based on the perpetual creation of the new. Technological innovations in both products and processes characterize our economic history over the last 200 years. This newness is always linked to uncertainty. Decisions must be taken in the present, but we cannot predict their outcomes. Herein lie opportunities but also risks. The dynamics of capitalism thus not only contains the enormous growth that has fundamentally transformed our societies, but also the recurring crises, most recently the 2008 financial crisis.

C: You regard expectations that arise under conditions of uncertainty as fictional. To what extent is irrationality involved here?

JB: Of course, economic actors try to calculate their decisions as accurately as possible. But behind many calculations lie assumptions that cannot themselves be calculated. One historical example makes this clear. Gottlieb Daimler once predicted that the German automobile market would not exceed one million vehicles, as there were simply no more chauffeurs. It never occurred to him that the cars' purchasers themselves would get behind the wheel. He conceived of the future as an extension of the past. Within the situation itself, we are unaware of the cultural influence of such calculations, an influence that would have to be glossed over to keep the narrative believable.

C: The capitalist economy expands our temporal horizon through the imaginary of the future. Can we say that in the economy everything is focused on the future?

JB: Yes, the modern world, of which the capitalist economy is a part, is completely focused on the future. Our actions in the present are motivated by ideas of the future. Every credit, every innovative project, but also our consumer habits, are characterized by this. In the case of consumption, this is known as "anticipatory consumption." In the modern world, the present and the past are repudiated. They are just a practiced reserve that feeds in part into the imaginaries of the future.

C: The sociologist Pierre Bourdieu regarded changes in the temporal order as a fixed component in capitalist development. Traditional societies saw the future as part of a circular repetition of events. In the temporal disposition of capitalism, the future is an open space that contains opportunities and risks. It is characteristic of capitalism that the actors believe in a future. How did modern capitalism's particular temporal disposition come about?

JB: Through cultural and institutional changes. In the Early Modern period, the Church lost its authority to interpret phenomena concerning the future. The future was seen as made by human beings. This is most clearly expressed in the narratives of progress created by the Enlightenment. At the same time, competition and the market were slowly emerging as allocation mechanisms in the economy. Competition forces economic actors to perceive the future as different from the present. Everyone knows that competitors strive to improve their position through innovations and that this is what undermines one's own position in the market, and one has to prepare for this with one's own innovations. Present-day forms have no future. It's useless: in capitalism you have to focus on the unknown future.

C: To what extent do promissory stories about technological developments influence society?

JB: Innovations exist in the first instance as ideas. In order to generate investments, actors must believe in the promises of innovation, and to do this, they use promissory stories. Artificial intelligence is a good example of this at the moment. In these technologies, a promising future is seen as something that is taken up and fueled by scientists, politicians, investors, and journalists. The state and the large research organizations mobilize funds, companies invest, and researchers focus on this sector. Initially, however, these are just promises. But the promises, to the extent that they are considered trustworthy, motivate the investments. Artificial intelligence is a good example, as there was already a hype about this sector in the 1960s—a hype that then completely petered out.

C: What are instruments of imagination?

JB: By instruments of imagination I mean the social technologies through which economic actors develop plausible narratives of the future. Let's take marketing. The job of marketing is to create an appetite among consumers for products they don't yet possess. This takes place through telling stories that trigger imaginaries of a future life with the product. Marketing promotes anticipatory consumption. But economic forecasts are also an instrument of imagination. Predicting growth rates, inflation, and unemployment for the following year allows economic actors to build a picture of the future economy—a future present on which they can focus their decisions. It doesn't matter that these projections are frequently wrong. They are simply replaced by new projections that in turn provide a focus for action.

C: If expectations underlie the dynamics of capitalism, what can stop these dynamics?

JB: Excessive uncertainty and lack of interest. If investments seem too uncertain in their results, this creates what Keynes once called "liquidity preference." Not enough is being invested and the economy falls short of its growth potential. On the demand side, lack of consumer interest would be fatal. If no one is interested in the latest version of the iPhone any more, or if people think it's enough to own just one pair of sneakers, the dynamics of growth are weakened.

C: Which ideas are the enemies of growth?

JB: Ironically, capitalism's counter-reactions have not destroyed it, rather they have been integrated into it. The labor movement gave rise to the welfare state, and in many respects this is simply a huge market. The hippie movement in California gave rise to Silicon Valley, and the ecological movement of the 1970s gave rise to renewable energy companies. When capitalism was criticized for its exploitation of developing countries, the fair-trade labels were created. It would be really dangerous for capitalism if no one was interested in all the innovations any more, if we were to say, we've had enough.

C: How important are narratives for a society in general?

JB: We can only approach the world by giving meaning to the sense impressions that we experience. Meaning as a whole is constructed through stories, or narratives, through which we create order out of events. The same goes for how we perceive the social interactions from which society is constituted, and how we regard the future. Without meaning both society and the economy do not exist.

C: By introducing the concept of fictional expectations, you have in mind a re-evaluation of Max Weber's observations on disenchantment in modern capitalism and the imprisonment of actors within an "iron cage." Can you tell us more?

JB: Generally speaking, we see the modern economy as the epitome of calculation and rationality. Max Weber also saw it this way and expressed it in his famous phrase about the modern world as being an "iron cage." But it is precisely when we want to understand the innovative and dynamic character of capitalism that this point of view reveals its limitations. Despite all the figures in its business plan, the innovative ideas of a start-up cannot be calculated rationally, but rather they are characterized by unsecured convictions and evocative excess. Joseph Schumpeter has a clear idea of this. For him, the entrepreneur is the person who pursues a project out of conviction, without being able to calculate the results. For him, the dynamics of capitalism have their foundations precisely in breaking out of the iron cage.

C: What are your hopes for capitalism today?

JB: I hope that the future of scientific and economic development might more fully reflect their consequences for the political community and for society as a whole. Here we might think both of the increasing social inequality in societies and of the consequences of smartphones for close social relationships. Where do we really want to go? I'm well aware that such a reflection on the desirable movement of society as a whole is at best wishful thinking in a functionally differentiated society. But you did ask me what my hopes are.

References

Jens Beckert, *Imagined Futures: Fictional Expectations and Capitalist Dynamics* (Cambridge MA: Harvard University Press, 2016).

Jens Beckert and Richard Brong (eds.), *Uncertain Futures. Imaginaries, Narratives and Calculation in the Economy* (Oxford: Oxford University Press, 2018).

CONTRIBUTORS

Prof. Dr. Lucio Baccaro has been Director at the Max Planck Institute for the Study of Societies in Cologne since 2017. His work as a political economist focuses on international comparative political economy from a sociological perspective. His current research interests include industrial relations, social policy, and the political economy of growth models. His most recent publication is *Trajectories of Neoliberal Transformation: European Industrial Relations since the 1970s* (Cambridge University Press, 2017), co-authored with Chris Howell. Lucio Baccaro gained his Ph.D. in 1997 at the University of Pavia in Italy and in 1999 at the Massachusetts Institute of Technology (MIT), and has held research posts at MIT and the International Labour Organization (ILO). Since 2009 he has been

Professor of Macrosociology at the University of Geneva.

Prof. Dr. Jens Beckert is Professor of Sociology and Director of the Max Planck Institute for the Study of Societies in Cologne. In 2018 he received the Leibniz Prize of the German Research Foundation (DFG). His latest book, *Imagined Futures. Fictional Expectations and Capitalist Dynamics* (2016), has just been published in German under the title *Imaginierte Zukunft. Fiktionale Erwartungen und die Dynamik des Kapitalismus* (2018).

Univ. Prof. em. Dr.sc. tc. hc. Bazon Brock, thinker at large and artist without portfolio, is Emeritus Professor of Aesthetics and Cultural Education at the Bergische Universität in Wuppertal, Germany. Other professorships include at Hamburg University of Fine Arts (1965–76) and the University of Applied Arts, Vienna (1977–80). In 1992 he was awarded an honorary doctorate at ETH (Swiss Federal Institute for Technology, Zürich) and in 2012 at the Hochschule für Gestaltung, Karlsruhe. Since 2014 he has been Honorary Professor for Prophecy at HBKsaar (Saar College of Fine Arts), Saarbrücken, and in 2016 he was awarded the Von der Heydt Prize by the City of Wuppertal. He has developed the method of "Action

Teaching," in which the seminar hall becomes a place of enactment, for oneself and others. Between 1968 and 1992, he led the documenta schools for visitors, which he founded in Kassel. From 2010 to 2013 he ran courses for "professional citizens" at the Karlsruhe University of Arts and Design. He has organized around 3,000 events and "action plays," most recently *Lustmarsch durchs Theoriegelände* (2006, in eleven museums). He is a member of the Institut für theoretische Kunst, Universalpoesie und Prognostik and Founder of the Amt für Arbeit an unlösbaren Problemen und Maßnahmen der hohen Hand, Berlin (www.denkerei-berlin.de).

Adam Curtis is a British documentary filmmaker. In his films he uses BBC archival footage through which he explores areas of sociology, psychology, philosophy, and political history. His main field of interest is power in society. Adam Curtis describes his work as journalism that is expressed via the medium of film. He has won four BAFTA Awards for his work. His films include among others *The Century of the Self* (2002), *The Power of Nightmares* (2004), *All Watched Over by Machines of Loving Grace* (2011), *Living in an Unreal World* (2016), and *HyperNormalisation* (2016).

Dr. Corinne Michaela Flick studied both law and literature, taking American studies as her subsidiary, at Ludwig Maximilian University, Munich. She gained her Dr. Phil. in 1989. She has worked as in-house lawyer for Bertelsmann Buch AG and Amazon.com. In 1998 she became General Partner in Vivil GmbH und Co. KG, Offenburg. She is Founder and Chair of the Convoco Foundation. As Editor of Convoco! Editions she has published the following volumes: *The Common Good in the 21st Century* (Convoco! Editions, 2018), *Authority in Transformation* (Convoco! Editions, 2017), *Power and its Paradoxes* (Convoco! Editions, 2016), *To Do or Not To Do—Inaction as a Form of Action* (Convoco! Editions, 2015), *Dealing with Downturns: Strategies in Uncertain Times* (Convoco! Editions, 2014), *Collective Lawbreaking—A Threat to Liberty* (Convoco! Editions, 2013), *Who Owns the World's Knowledge?* (Convoco! Editions, 2012), *Staatsfinanzierung und Wirtschaftsfinanzierung am Scheideweg* (FVA, 2010), *Das demographische Problem als Gefahr für Rechtskultur und Wirtschaft* (FVA, 2009). In 2018, Corinne Flick became the Chair of the Board of Ambassadors at the ESMT Berlin.

Sean Hagan was General Counsel of the International Monetary Fund from 2004 until September 2018. He is currently Visiting Fellow at Exeter College, Oxford University. While at the IMF, Sean Hagan was responsible for all legal matters pertaining to the IMF's regulatory, financial, and advisory services. He led the IMF's recent efforts to overhaul its approach to addressing corruption. He has published extensively on the law of the IMF and on issues pertaining to the prevention and resolution of financial crises. Prior to joining the IMF, Sean Hagan was in private practice, first in New York and subsequently in Tokyo.

Prof. Dr. Kai A. Konrad is Director at the Max Planck Institute for Tax Law and Public Finance and a Scientific Member of the Max Planck Society. He was a Full Professor of Economics at the Freie Universität Berlin from 1994 to 2009, and from 2001 to 2009 he was a Director at the Wissenschaftszentrum Berlin für Sozialforschung (WZB). He is a member of the German National Academy of Sciences Leopoldina and of four other science academies. He is a co-editor of the *Journal of Public Economics*. Since 1999 he has been a member of the Council of Scientific Advisors to the Federal Ministry of Finance and was the Chair from 2011 to 2014.

Prof. Dr. Stefan Korioth gained his doctorate in law in 1990 and completed his postdoctoral qualification in public and constitutional law. From 1996 to 2000 he was Professor of Public Law, Constitutional History, and Theory of Government at Greifswald. In 2000 he accepted the Chair of Public and Ecclesiastical Law at Ludwig Maximilian University Munich. His publications include *Integration und Bundesstaat* (1990), *Der Finanzausgleich zwischen Bund und Ländern* (1997), *Grundzüge des Staatskirchenrechts* (with B. Jean d'Heur, 2000), *Das Bundesverfassungsgericht* (with Klaus Schlaich, 11th edition, 2018), and *Staatsrecht I – Staatsorganisationsrecht* (4th edition, 2018).

Prof. Justin Yifu Lin, Ph.D. is Dean of the Institute of New Structural Economics and the Institute of South-South Cooperation and Development and Professor and Honorary Dean of the National School of Development at Peking University. He was the Senior Vice-President and Chief Economist of the World Bank from 2008 to 2012. Prior to this, Prof. Lin served for 15 years as Founding Director and Professor of the China Centre for Economic Research (CCER) at Peking University. He is a councilor on the State Council and a member of the Standing Committee, Chinese People's Political Consultation Conference. He is the author of more than 20 books including *Beating the Odds: Jump-starting Developing Countries* (2017), *Going Beyond Aid: Development Cooperation for Structural Transformation* (2016), *The Quest for Prosperity: How Developing Economies Can Take Off* (2012), *New Structural Economics: A Framework for Rethinking Development and Policy* (2010), *Against the Consensus: Reflections on the Great Recession* (2013), and *Demystifying the Chinese Economy* (2011). He is a Corresponding Fellow of the British Academy and a member of the Academy of Sciences for the Developing World.

Prof. Dr. h.c. Rudolf Mellinghoff is President of the Federal Fiscal Court. He studied at the University of Münster and served his postgraduate legal internship in Baden-Württemberg. Between 1984 and 1987 he was a Research Assistant at the University of Heidelberg, becoming a Judge in the Finance Court of Düsseldorf in 1987. From 1987 to 1991 he was a Research Fellow at the Federal Constitutional Court. He was appointed Judge at the Finance Court of Düsseldorf in 1989. Rudolf Mellinghoff was Head of Department at the Ministry of Justice of Mecklenburg-Vorpommern between July 1991 and June 1992, and was appointed Presiding Judge of the Finance Court in 1996. In a second full-time position, he served as Judge of the Higher Administrative

Court of Mecklenburg-Vorpommern between 1992 and 1996. From 1995 to 1996 he was also a member of the Constitutional Court of Mecklenburg-Vorpommern, and from 1997 to 2001 served as Judge at the Federal Supreme Finance Court. From January 2001 to October 2011 Rudolf Mellinghoff served as Justice in the Second Senate of the Federal Constitutional Court. Since then he has been President of the Federal Supreme Court of Finance. In 2006 Rudolf Mellinghoff was awarded an Honorary Doctorate from the University of Greifswald, and in 2007 from the Eberhard Karls University in Tübingen. In 2011 he was awarded the Grand Merit Cross with Star and Sash of the Order of Merit of the Federal Republic of Germany. He is currently Vice Chair of the Deutsche Steuerjuristische Gesellschaft and Chair of the Advisory Council of the Berliner Steuergespräche e.V. He is a member of the Judicial Integrity Group, and from 2009 to 2011 was President of the German Section of the International Commission of Jurists, becoming Vice-President in 2012.

Prof. Dr. Timo Meynhardt holds the Dr. Arend Oetker Chair of Business Psychology and Leadership at the HHL Leipzig Graduate School of Management. He is Managing Director of the Center for Leadership and Values in Society at the University of St. Gallen, where he obtained his doctorate and postdoctoral qualification in business administration. For several years, he was Practice Expert at McKinsey & Company. Timo Meynhardt's work focuses on public value management, leadership and competency diagnostics, combining psychology and business management in his research and teaching. He publishes the *Public Value Atlas* for Switzerland and Germany, which aims at making transparent the social benefits of companies and organizations (www.gemeinwohlatlas.de, www. gemeinwohl.ch). His Public Value Scorecard provides a management tool to measure and analyze the creation of public value. He is also Patron of the EY Public Value Awards for Startups (www.eypva.com).

Hans Ulrich Obrist is the Artistic Director of the Serpentine Galleries, London, and co-founder of 89plus. Prior to this, he was Curator of the Musée d'Art Moderne de la Ville de Paris. Since his first show "World Soup (The Kitchen Show)" in 1991, he has curated more than 300 exhibitions. Obrist has lectured internationally at academic and art institutions, and is a contributing editor to the magazines *Artforum*, *AnOther Magazine*, *032C*, a regular contributor to *Mousse* and *Kaleidoscope* and he writes columns for *Das Magazin* and *Weltkunst*. In 2011 he received the CCS

Bard Award for Curatorial Excellence, and in 2015 he was awarded the International Folkwang Prize for his commitment to the arts. His recent publications include *Mondialité* (2018), *Conversations in Mexico* (2016), *The Age of Earthquakes* with Douglas Coupland and Shumon Basar (2015), and *Ways of Curating* (2014).

Dr. Stefan Oschmann has been Chairman of the Executive Board and CEO of Merck since 2016. Prior to that, he served as Vice-Chairman and Deputy CEO, with responsibility for group strategy, among other things. He joined Merck in 2011 as a member of the Executive Board and was responsible for the health-care business sector until the end of 2014. He drove the transformation of biopharma business and played an instrumental role in the group-wide transformation and growth program "Fit for 2018." Before joining Merck, Stefan Oschmann worked for the US pharmaceutical company MSD. He started his career at an agency of the United Nations, and also worked for the German Chemical Industry Association (VCI). He holds a doctorate in veterinary medicine from Ludwig Maximilian University, Munich.

Prof. Dr. Christoph G. Paulus studied law at Munich, taking his doctorate in law in 1980. His post-doctoral qualification, gained in 1991, was in civil law, civil procedure, and Roman law, for which he was awarded the Medal of the University of Paris II. Between 1989 and 1990 he was a recipient of a Feodor Lynen Stipend from the Humboldt Foundation in Berkeley, from which he had earlier gained his LL.M. From 1992 to 1994 he was Associate Professor at Augsburg, and from the summer semester 1994 he was at the Law Faculty of Humboldt University in Berlin, becoming Dean of the Faculty 2008–10. He is Consultant to the International Monetary Fund and the World Bank. Among other roles, he is a member of the International Insolvency Institute of the American College of Bankruptcy and the International Association for Procedural Law. From 2006 to 2010 he was advisor on insolvency law to the German delegation to UNCITRAL. He is on the editorial board of the *Zeitschrift für Wirtschaftsrecht* (ZIP), the *Norton Annual Review of International Insolvency*, and the *International Insolvency Law Review*.

Prof. Dr. Herbert A. Reitsamer is a communications engineer, Professor of Neuro- and Sensory Physiology, and Professor of Ophthalmology. He is Chairman of the University Eye Clinic and the University Clinic in Salzburg, and Head of the Research Program in Experimental Ophthalmology at Paracelsus Medical University. He is Chairman of the Professorial Committee at the University of Salzburg, a member of the Austrian Supreme Health Council, a member of Salzburg's Ethics Committee, and Executive Board member of the Austrian Ophthalmological Society. Prof. Reitsamer is a member of the European Academy of Sciences and President of the Austrian Chapter Affiliate of the American Association for Research in Vision and Ophthalmology. He is also a member of numerous advisory boards in universities, start-ups, and industrial enterprises; a member of editorial boards; and acts as referee for scientific journals and funding institutions.

Prof. Dr. Albrecht Ritschl is Professor at the Economic History Department at the London School of Economics. After his doctorate and postdoctoral qualification at the University of Munich, he became Associate Professor at the Universitat Pompeu Fabra in Barcelona, followed by chairs at the University of Zurich, and the Humboldt University of Berlin. Albrecht Ritschl is a member of the Board of Academic Advisors of the German Federal Ministry for Economic Affairs as well as Fellow at the Centre for Economic Policy Research (CEPR), the Centre for Economic Performance (CEP), and the CESifo. He has authored many publications on the economic history of the 20th century, in particular on Germany during the financial crisis and the rise of National Socialism. His warnings concerning a strict deflation policy during the Greek debt crisis and its parallels to the German deflation policy during the global economic crisis gained wide recognition. Albrecht Ritschl was spokesperson for a history committee at the German Federal Ministry for Economic Affairs. Currently, he is coordinating a project on the history of the German Reichsbank and the German Central Bank.

Prof. Jörg Rocholl, Ph.D. is President of the ESMT Berlin and a member of the Economic Advisory Board of the German Federal Ministry of Finance. In addition, he is Chairman of the Research Council of the Research Data and Service Centre of the Federal Bank of Germany, Vice-Chairman of the Economic Advisory Board of Deutsche Welle, a member of the Scientific Advisory Board of the DIW Berlin, Research Professor at the ifo Institute in Munich, Duisenberg Fellow of the European Central Bank (ECB), and research member of the European Corporate Governance Institute (ECGI). Jörg Rocholl studied economy at the Witten/Herdecke University where he graduated with distinction. Afterwards, he completed his Ph.D. at Colombia University in New York and was appointed to his first position as Assistant Professor at the University of North Carolina in Chapel Hill. Since 2007 Jörg Rocholl has taught and engaged in research at the ESMT, where he has been President since 2011. In 2010, he was awarded the EY Chair in Governance and Compliance.

Gisbert Rühl has been CEO of the corporation Klöckner & Co since 2005 after having held several leading positions in industry and in consulting. He was initially Financial Manager, and since 2009 he has been Chairman of the Executive Board. Currently, Gisbert Rühl is advancing the digital transformation of Klöckner & Co as well as the development of an independent industry platform, XOM Materials, in which the company plays a pioneering role in the industry.

Prof. Dr. Monika Schnitzer holds the Chair for Comparative Economics at the Ludwig Maximilian University, Munich. In her research, Monika Schnitzer deals with innovation, competition, and multinational companies. She received her doctorate and postdoctoral qualification at the University of Bonn and she has been Visiting Professor at Boston University, MIT, Stanford University, Yale University, University of California, Berkeley, and Harvard University. Since May 2011 she has been Deputy Chairwoman of the Commission of Experts for Research and Innovation. Previously, she was a member of the Economic Advisory Group on Competition Policy of the Directorate-General for Competition of the European Commission. In addition, she is a member of the Scientific Advisory Council of the Federal Ministry for Economic Affairs and Energy and of the Bayerische Akademie der Wissenschaften (Bavarian Academy of Sciences). In 2015–16 she served as President of the Verein für Socialpolitik (German Economic Association).

Prof. Dr. Dr. h.c. Wolfgang Schön was awarded his doctorate of law at the University of Bonn in 1985, and in 1992 he received his postdoctoral qualification there. He was Professor at the University of Bielefeld from 1992 to 1996, and from 1996 to 2002 was again at

Bonn. Since 2002 he has been Director and Scientific Member of the Max Planck Institute for Intellectual Property, Competition, and Tax Law in Munich. He is Honorary Professor at Ludwig Maximilian University Munich; member of the Global Law Faculty, New York University; and International Research Fellow, University of Oxford Centre of Business Taxation. From 2008 to 2014 Prof. Schön was Vice-President of the Max Planck Society. Since 2014 he has been Vice-President of the German Research Foundation (DFG). He has published numerous works on company law, competition law, and tax law.

THE COMMON GOOD IN THE 21ST CENTURY
2018

ISBN: 978-0-9931953-6-5

With contributions by: Roland Berger, Bazon Brock, Udo Di Fabio, Carl Benedikt Frey, Clemens Fuest, Kai A. Konrad, Stefan Korioth, Rudolf Mellinghoff, Timo Meynhardt, Hans Ulrich Obrist with Hito Steyerl and Matteo Pasquinelli, Stefan Oschmann, Christoph G. Paulus, Jörg Rocholl, Wolfgang Schön, Jens Spahn

AUTHORITY IN TRANSFORMATION
2017

ISBN: 978-0-9931953-4-1

With contributions by: Claudia Buch, Clemens Fuest, Thomas Hoeren, Peter M. Huber, Kai A. Konrad, Stefan Korioth, Peter Maurer, Hans Ulrich Obrist and Richard Wentworth, Stefan Oschmann, Christoph G. Paulus, Roger Scruton, Wolfgang Schön

POWER AND ITS PARADOXES

2016

ISBN: 978-0-9931953-2-7

With contributions by: Clemens Fuest, Thomas Hoeren, Wolfgang Ischinger, Stefan Korioth, Hans Ulrich Obrist and Simon Denny, Christoph G. Paulus, Albrecht Ritschl, Jörg Rocholl, Roger Scruton, Brendan Simms

TO DO OR NOT TO DO—INACTION AS A FORM OF ACTION

2015

ISBN: 978-0-9931953-0-3

With contributions by: Bazon Brock, Gert-Rudolf Flick, Peter M. Huber, Kai A. Konrad, Stefan Korioth, Friedhelm Mennekes, Hans Ulrich Obrist and Marina Abramović, Christoph G. Paulus, Jörg Rocholl, Wolfgang Schön, Roger Scruton, Pirmin Stekeler-Weithofer

DEALING WITH DOWNTURNS: STRATEGIES IN UNCERTAIN TIMES
2014

ISBN: 978-0-9572958-8-9

With contributions by: Jens Beckert, Bazon Brock, Saul David, Gerd Gigerenzer, Paul Kirchhof, Kai A. Konrad, Stefan Korioth, Christoph G. Paulus, Jörg Rocholl, Burkhard Schwenker

COLLECTIVE LAW-BREAKING—A THREAT TO LIBERTY
2013

ISBN: 978-0-9572958-5-8

With contributions by: Shaukat Aziz, Roland Berger, Christoph G. Paulus, Ingolf Pernice, Wolfgang Schön, Hannes Siegrist, Jürgen Stark, Pirmin Stekeler-Weithofer

WHO OWNS THE WORLD'S KNOWLEDGE?
2012

ISBN: 978-0-9572958-0-3

With contributions by: Eckhard Cordes, Urs Gasser, Thomas Hoeren, Viktor Mayer-Schönberger, Christoph G. Paulus, Jürgen Renn, Burkhard Schwenker, Hannes Siegrist

CAN'T PAY, WON'T PAY? SOVEREIGN DEBT AND THE CHALLENGE OF GROWTH IN EUROPE
2011

ISBN: 978-0-9572958-3-4

With contributions by: Roland Berger, Howard Davies, Otmar Issing, Paul Kirchhof, Kai A. Konrad, Stefan Korioth, Christoph G. Paulus, Burkhard Schwenker